New Day

Edited by Naomi Starkey January–April 2011

The Bible Reading Fellowship
15 The Chambers, Vineyard, Abingdon OX14 3FE
Tel: 01865 319700; Fax: 01865 319701
E-mail: enquiries@brf.org.uk; Website: www.brf.org.uk

ISBN 978 1 84101 625 2

Distributed in Australia by Willow Connection, PO Box 288, Brookvale, NSW 2100.
Tel: 02 9948 3957; Fax: 02 9948 8153;
E-mail: info@willowconnection.com.au
Available also from all good Christian bookshops in Australia.
For individual and group subscriptions in Australia:
Mrs Rosemary Morrall, PO Box W35, Wanniassa, ACT 2903.

Distributed in New Zealand by Scripture Union Wholesale, PO Box 760, Wellington
Tel: 04 385 0421; Fax: 04 384 3990; E-mail: suwholesale@clear.net.nz

Publications distributed to more than 60 countries

Acknowledgments

Printed in Singapore by Craft Print International Ltd

Suggestions for using *New Daylight*

Find a regular time and place, if possible, where you can read and pray undisturbed. Before you begin, take time to be still and perhaps use the BRF prayer. Then read the Bible passage slowly (try reading it aloud if you find it over-familiar), followed by the comment. You can also use *New Daylight* for group study and discussion, if you prefer.

The prayer or point for reflection can be a starting point for your own meditation and prayer. Many people like to keep a journal to record their thoughts about a Bible passage and items for prayer. In *New Daylight* we also note the Sundays and some special festivals from the Church calendar, to keep in step with the Christian year.

New Daylight and the Bible

New Daylight contributors use a range of Bible versions, and you will find a list of the versions used in each issue opposite, on page 2. You are welcome to use your own preferred version alongside the passage printed in the notes, and this can be particularly helpful if the Bible text has been abridged.

New Daylight affirms that the whole of the Bible is God's revelation to us, and we should read, reflect on and learn from every part of both Old and New Testaments. Usually the printed comment presents a straightforward 'thought for the day', but sometimes it may also raise questions rather than simply providing answers, as we wrestle with some of the more difficult passages of Scripture.

New Daylight *is also available in a deluxe edition (larger format). Check out your local Christian bookshop or contact the BRF office, who can also give more details about a cassette version for the visually impaired. For a Braille edition, contact St John's Guild, 8 St Raphael's Court, Avenue Road, St Albans, AL1 3EH.*

Writers in this issue

Maggi Dawn began her career as a singer-songwriter and later studied theology at Cambridge, where she is now Chaplain and Fellow at Robinson College. Her two BRF books include the 2010 Lent book *Giving It Up*. Her latest publication is *The Writing on the Wall* (Hodder, 2010).

Tony Horsfall is a freelance trainer and retreat leader based in Yorkshire, with his own ministry, Charis Training. He is an elder of Ackworth Community Church and has written several books for BRF, including *Mentoring for Spiritual Growth* and *Working from a Place of Rest*.

Naomi Starkey is a Commissioning Editor for BRF and edits and writes for *New Daylight* Bible reading notes. She has also written *Good Enough Mother* (BRF, 2009).

Andrew John has been the Bishop of Bangor since 2008, having previously ministered in the Diocese of St Davids. He is married to Caroline, who is also a deacon in the Church in Wales, and they have four children.

Amy Boucher Pye is an American who has lived in the UK for over a decade. She makes her home in North London with her husband and young family and enjoys writing for Christian periodicals.

Veronica Zundel is an Oxford graduate, writer and journalist. She lives with her husband and son in North London, where they belong to the Mennonite Church.

Michael Mitton is a freelance writer, trainer and consultant. He is also the Derby Diocesan Adviser for Fresh Expressions and Priest in Charge of St Paul's, Derby. He worked previously for Anglican Renewal Ministries and the Acorn Christian Healing Foundation.

David Winter is retired from parish ministry. An honorary Canon of Christ Church, Oxford, he is well known as a writer and broadcaster. His most recent book for BRF is *Pilgrim's Way*.

Dick France is an Anglican minister who taught New Testament at two universities in Nigeria and at the London School of Theology. He was Principal of Wycliffe Hall, Oxford and then served as Rector of seven small parishes on the Welsh border until retirement.

Margaret Silf is an ecumenical Christian, committed to working across and beyond the denominational divides. She devotes herself to writing and accompanying others on their spiritual journey.

Naomi Starkey writes...

Welcome to *New Daylight* 2011, the year when the 400th anniversary of the King James Version is celebrated! Over the coming months, this momentous event in the history of scripture translation will be commemorated nationally and we will be including a linked series of readings in the September–December issue of the notes.

As well as noting the historical significance, we can use this anniversary as a reminder of the importance not only of reading the Bible but of ensuring that our work continues to bring its message to our rapidly changing culture. BRF is also involved in *Biblefresh*, an initiative bringing together churches, Christian agencies, colleges and festivals working to encourage a greater confidence in the Bible across the UK.

You may be aware that *New Daylight* was launched as an iPhone application last year, with a rapid take-up across the world. The rise of the Internet has been likened to the invention of the printing press in its revolutionary potential for daily life and it is exciting to think that technological advances can continue to help people grow in faith. The message of the Bible can be conveyed in many different ways—wonderful though it is, there is nothing intrinsically sacred about the printed page! If you have not done so before (or recently), do visit the BRF website (www.brf.org.uk) to see how we are exploring the ways new media can extend our ministry to people we wouldn't otherwise be able to meet.

Turning to this issue, I would like to welcome four new contributors. Beginning the year, we have readings from the Psalms by Maggi Dawn, whose name will be familiar to many from her BRF Advent and Lent books. R.T. (Dick) France, who provides our Easter readings, wrote a couple of volumes for the *People's Bible Commentary* series, while Michael Mitton has also written books for BRF, including *A Heart to Listen*. His first *New Daylight* notes take a fresh look at the story of Joseph, while Andrew John, Bishop of Bangor, joins us to write two weeks reflecting on 1 John.

Finally, thanks once again to everyone who has been in touch with words of encouragement or challenge for us. We always value hearing from our readers and hope that you will continue to find the notes helpful as 2011 unfolds.

The BRF Prayer

Almighty God,

you have taught us that your word is a lamp for our feet and a light for our path. Help us, and all who prayerfully read your word, to deepen our fellowship with each other through your love. And in so doing may we come to know you more fully, love you more truly, and follow more faithfully in the steps of your son Jesus Christ, who lives and reigns with you and the Holy Spirit, one God for evermore. Amen.

Praying with Psalms 75—77

In 1 Chronicles 6:1, we find a long list of the descendants of Levi—the tribe with priestly and liturgical responsibilities. Verse 16 names Gershom, Kohath and Merari, founders of the three great families descended from Levi, son of Jacob. Kohath's grandson, Korah, began an insurrection against Moses and Aaron's leadership (Numbers 16), but his descendants became the great musicians of ancient Israelite worship. If you read the titles of the psalms you will notice that a number of them are attributed to the Sons of Korah, one of whom—18 generations after Korah—was Heman the singer, who worked side by side with his relative, Asaph: 'These are the men whom David put in charge of the service of song in the house of the Lord... Of the Kohathites: Heman, the singer... and his brother Asaph, who stood on his right' (1 Chronicles 6:31, 33, 39).

The name of Asaph appears throughout the first book of Chronicles as a musician, songwriter, arranger of music and conductor of worship in Jerusalem. He was often left in charge of musical and liturgical affairs and, in particular, had the responsibility of looking after the ark of the covenant (1 Chronicles 16:37)—that uniquely significant and holy piece of furniture in pre-temple Israelite worship. In later years, Asaph's sons followed him in this musical tradition.

Genealogies and historical connections are notoriously difficult to establish with any particular certainty in the Old Testament, so it is impossible to be sure whether the psalms attributed to David, the Sons of Korah, Asaph and others were actually written by them or composed at later points in Israel's history and then named after these heroes of the musical tradition.

Twelve of the psalms (numbers 50 and 73—83) are known as the Psalms of Asaph and we shall be working through three of them during the next eight days. Psalms 75—77 seem to fit best into later periods in Israel's history, but, despite the fact that we cannot be certain of their authorship, we can appreciate their beauty. They capture how their author(s) managed to live with faith and doubt, fear and relief, anger and rejoicing and through the turmoil of some extreme life events.

Maggi Dawn

PSALM 75:1–3 (NRSV)

To sing is to pray twice

> To the leader: Do Not Destroy. A Psalm of Asaph. A Song. We give thanks to you, O God; we give thanks; your name is near. People tell of your wondrous deeds. At the set time that I appoint I will judge with equity. When the earth totters, with all its inhabitants, it is I who keep its pillars steady.

Before getting into the psalm itself, it is worth pausing to note the title: 'Do Not Destroy. A Psalm of Asaph. A Song.' Hymn books are usually indexed by author and first line, but also by metre (number of syllables per line) and tune—for instance, 'Dear Lord and Father' will be followed by 'Words: Whittier, 1872, Music: Repton, Parry, Meter: 86 886.' It appears that, at some point, the Psalms were named and catalogued in a similar way. 'Do Not Destroy' is thought to be the name of the tune, while Asaph is named as author. Also, the psalm is specified, not as a poem, a reading, a prayer or a musical interlude, but a song.

As Augustine wrote, 'To sing is to pray twice.' Psychologists and music theorists have found it hard to explain precisely why music expresses things more profoundly than words, but few would dispute that it is the case. Approaching any study of Psalms, it is well worth pausing to bear in mind that we are reading the lyrics of songs, to which the music has been lost.

Song lyrics are not exactly the same as poetry, but what they have in common is that they rely for their meaning as much on the sound and the rhythm of the words, and the emotive quality of the phrasing, as they do on meaning that could be re-expressed as reasoned argument. That does not mean that they are simply beautiful and untrue, but it does mean that they approach truth in a different way. A song is not meant to deliver doctrine in rational statements, but it can express some truths far better than theology. That is, some things can be 'said' better through music than words and the Psalms need to be read with that idea in mind.

Reflection

As we read the Psalms, may our hearts and minds be opened to their musical quality.

MD

Sunday 2 January

PSALM 75:2–3 (NRSV)

Great is thy faithfulness

At the set time that I appoint I will judge with equity. When the earth totters, with all its inhabitants, it is I who keep its pillars steady.

Psalm 75 celebrates a narrow escape from an enemy. It appears, at first sight, to be the reply to the near-despair of the previous psalm, which was probably written during the devastation of the Babylonian exile in 586BC. The question, 'Why do bad things happen to good people?' is often cited as the greatest stumbling block to faith, but Psalm 74 asks the opposite: 'Why do good things happen to bad people?' It's full of anger at the exiles' plight—anger at their enemies, at themselves for not preventing their doom and a desperate plea to God, wondering why the enemy is getting away with it.

Psalm 75, then, follows as a song of thankful relief—but it is thought to have been written 150 to 200 years earlier than Psalm 74, in a completely different set of circumstances. Not long after Hezekiah became King of Judah, he was threatened by Sennacherib, the bloodthirsty king of Assyria. Hezekiah paid him a huge bribe to avoid an attack, but Sennacherib returned and besieged the city. Jerusalem must have been quaking with fear, knowing the merciless reputation of the Assyrians. In 2 Kings 18–19, 2 Chronicles 32, and Isaiah 36—37, however, it is recorded that, the night before their attack, the entire Assyrian army was 'struck down'—perhaps by an outbreak of cholera—and the people of Jerusalem recovered their treasures from among the dead. The Assyrian account (on the Sennacherib Prism, c. 690BC) is quite different, claiming that the Assyrians returned home victorious with the wealth of Jerusalem, and it's hard to tell which account is more historically correct. Whatever the precise details, Jerusalem went, overnight, from facing destruction to being completely off the hook and the waves of relief in Psalm 75 are palpable.

Even though Psalms 74 and 75 are historically disjointed, placed side by side they are a reminder that, although life is unpredictable and our emotions can be a roller coaster, God holds the foundations steady.

Prayer

Let us pray, in good times and bad, that we may perceive God's faithfulness to us.

MD

Psalm 75:4–10 (NRSV)

God is not vengeful

I say to the boastful, 'Do not boast', and to the wicked, 'Do not lift up your horn; do not lift up your horn on high, or speak with insolent neck.' For not from the east or from the west and not from the wilderness comes lifting up; but it is God who executes judgment, putting down one and lifting up another. For in the hand of the Lord there is a cup with foaming wine, well mixed; he will pour a draught from it, and all the wicked of the earth shall drain it down to the dregs. But I will rejoice for ever; I will sing praises to the God of Jacob. All the horns of the wicked I will cut off, but the horns of the righteous shall be exalted.

These verses celebrate God's vindication of the psalmist and his people in their battles against their enemies. The Psalms contain some of the most emotionally unrestrained writings in the Bible and sometimes the cry for vengeance to be meted out on enemies clashes with the ideals of forgiveness and mercy. So, it can be difficult to know how to assimilate such passages into our understanding, but two things from this one are helpful. One is the reminder that 'it is God who executes judgment'. Although we, like the psalmist, can and should express anger at injustice, we should not stray into vengeance. The other is the image of the foaming cup, drained to the dregs. This does not mean a potion brewed up by God to punish the wicked, nor a tit-for-tat punishment, but a deep fracture in the goodness of the universe that affects everyone.

The Psalms of Asaph ask why God does not make life fair, but the answer is that the consequences of evil and injustice are indiscriminate in their devastation. The imagery is repeated in Gethsemane, where Jesus implores his Father to 'remove this cup from me' (Luke 22:42); at Golgotha, he drank it to its dregs. In Revelation 14, too, the apostate will 'drink the wine of God's wrath' (v. 10). The cup is not something prepared for those who deserve it, but a reminder that evil has its consequences for everyone, even for those who stand up against it.

Reflection

'Weeping may linger for a night, but joy comes with the morning' (Psalm 30:5).

MD

PSALM 76:1–6 (NRSV)

God is with us (but not on 'our side')

To the leader: with stringed instruments. A Psalm of Asaph. A Song. In Judah God is known, his name is great in Israel. His abode has been established in Salem, his dwelling-place in Zion. There he broke the flashing arrows, the shield, the sword, and the weapons of war. Glorious are you, more majestic than the everlasting mountains. The stout-hearted were stripped of their spoil; they sank into sleep; none of the troops was able to lift a hand. At your rebuke, O God of Jacob, both rider and horse lay stunned.

It seems that Psalm 76 was written, or reappropriated, following Hezekiah's escape from the Assyrian siege (see 2 January). As such, it belongs with Psalm 75. It opens with two grand themes. First, that God is famous because he saved Jerusalem. Jerusalem became invincible, not because of human power or ingenuity, but against the odds. God is renowned not purely for being transcendent and beyond comprehension but also because of his connection with his people. There is a tremendous beauty to the exploration of Christian theology, but a beautiful theology is not enough to sustain faith every day—we need a sense that God is not just 'out there' but also with us.

The second theme is one of the most difficult to negotiate in the Psalms because it makes the tragedy that befalls other people a cause for celebration. For the psalmist, the uncomplicated truth was that the people of God had been threatened and their escape from disaster was cause for a song of victory. Nowadays, of course, we consider it uncivilised to rejoice over the tragedies of war. One of the lessons of the past century—as technological advances have made it increasingly possible to see the world from other people's points of view—is that God is not on anyone's 'side', but on the side of justice, peace and goodness. Perhaps the only way to make sense of these difficult passages in the Psalms is to acknowledge that they are of their time. What remains unchanged, though, is the belief that God is against injustice and evil, but we should avoid the implication that God is against people.

Reflection

May we find the threads of faith in these words
yet also appreciate their ancient context.

MD

PSALM 76:7–12 (NRSV)

A tale of two kings

> But you indeed are awesome! Who can stand before you when once your anger is roused? From the heavens you uttered judgment; the earth feared and was still when God rose up to establish judgment, to save all the oppressed of the earth. Human wrath serves only to praise you, when you bind the last bit of your wrath around you. Make vows to the Lord your God, and perform them; let all who are around him bring gifts to the one who is awesome, who cuts off the spirit of princes, who inspires fear in the kings of the earth.

Today is the eve of Epiphany, when the Western Church celebrates the coming of the magi, or, wise men (Matthew 2:1–12). The Christian writer Tertullian (born C. AD160) linked them with some Old Testament prophecies referring to foreign kings bringing gifts to the Messiah (Psalms 68:29; 72:10) and so renamed them magi-kings. His contemporary, Origen, imagined that, as they brought three gifts, there must have been three kings, while Irenaeus of Lyons suggested that the gifts represented Christ's roles—gold for a king, frankincense for a deity and myrrh to foretell his death.

Psalm 76, a story of a standoff between two kings—Hezekiah and Sennacherib—also reflects on human power at home and abroad, recognising the greater authority of God. Hezekiah had become lazy in his religious observance and it was the crisis of the siege that woke him up, while Sennacherib (as the Bible tells it) had to acknowledge that he was no match for the God of Israel.

'Human wrath serves only to praise you'—there is a resonance here with the Beatitudes (Matthew 5:1–12), in that, whatever the substance of human disagreements, love and grace will prevail. Whether we come in power or weakness, in submission like the magi or in pride like Sennacherib, everything is, in the end, subject to God's love and mercy. It is not God's wrath that brings order, but his enduring goodness.

Reflection

'Blessed are you when people revile you and persecute you and utter all kinds of evil against you falsely on my account. Rejoice and be glad, for your reward is great in heaven' (Matthew 5:11–12).

MD

Psalm 77:1–9 (NRSV)

Forgotten by God?

To the leader: according to Jeduthun. Of Asaph. A Psalm. I cry aloud to God, aloud to God, that he may hear me. In the day of my trouble I seek the Lord; in the night my hand is stretched out without wearying; my soul refuses to be comforted. I think of God, and I moan; I meditate, and my spirit faints. You keep my eyelids from closing; I am so troubled that I cannot speak. I consider the days of old, and remember the years of long ago. I commune with my heart in the night; I meditate and search my spirit: 'Will the Lord spurn for ever, and never again be favourable? Has his steadfast love ceased for ever? Are his promises at an end for all time? Has God forgotten to be gracious? Has he in anger shut up his compassion?'

This is one of three psalms (39, 62 and 77) linked to Jeduthun, one of the tabernacle choirmasters during David's reign. Each one seeks God's wisdom and is intensely personal. This psalm is clearly the prayer of someone well into middle age.

We might expect that the longer we live in faith, the closer God is, but it seems the opposite experience is common, that people who have lived a lifetime of faith suddenly feel that God is remote. Gregory of Nyssa (c. 330–c. 395) believed that the closer we get to God, the more we become aware of his otherness and lose the youthful confidence that made clarity so easy to come by.

The psalmist asserts (vv. 1–3) that he will continue to pray even though God seems far away. Then he says that, through sleepless nights of nostalgic longing for the good old days, his faith has been shaken. Where is God now? Has he stopped loving us? These are like C.S. Lewis' questions in *A Grief Observed* (1961)—is there no God, or (and this would be even worse) is it the truth that God *is* there, but he is not good after all?

Reflection

Sometimes we need to look our doubts and questions in the face.
If we have not felt God's presence for a long time, we can admit it,
say it aloud and wait for God's answer.

MD

Psalm 77:10–15 (NRSV)

Sing in the darkness

And I say, 'It is my grief that the right hand of the Most High has changed.' I will call to mind the deeds of the Lord; I will remember your wonders of old. I will meditate on all your work, and muse on your mighty deeds. Your way, O God, is holy. What god is so great as our God? You are the God who works wonders; you have displayed your might among the peoples. With your strong arm you redeemed your people, the descendants of Jacob and Joseph.

When we are in the midst of doubt, it is pointless to pretend that we are not. Faith, though, is not defined by how we think and feel in one particular moment but in what unfolds as the principles of our entire life. In response to the doubts in the first half of his song, the psalmist not only calls his faith to mind, but sings out loud about it. He remembers what he has always held to be true and this becomes the backdrop against which he can assess his current situation.

Someone once told me that the worst time to make decisions is in a time of trauma. 'Wait till the storm has passed,' he said, 'before you decide whether or not to rethink your faith.' Faith is as much about being faithful as it is to holding a conviction and, when we're plagued with doubts, holding on to the bigger picture is the smart thing to do.

That is easy to say, of course. One of the hardest things to do is sing in the darkness, but there are good reasons for doing so. One is that singing is a proven remedy for depression—partly due to the beauty of the music, but mostly because singing makes you stand up straight, breathe deeply and get a rush of oxygen to the bloodstream. Another reason is that singing familiar songs can reinforce the threads that run through our lives, giving us a sense of continuity and purpose. In the case of psalms and hymns, it is the thread of faith that is reinforced.

Reflection

When faith seems thin or unreal, 'I will call to mind the deeds of the Lord; I will remember your wonders of old.'

MD

Saturday 8 January

Psalm 77:16–20 (NRSV)

A community of faith

When the waters saw you, O God, when the waters saw you, they were afraid; the very deep trembled. The clouds poured out water; the skies thundered; your arrows flashed on every side. The crash of your thunder was in the whirlwind; your lightnings lit up the world; the earth trembled and shook. Your way was through the sea, your path, through the mighty waters; yet your footprints were unseen. You led your people like a flock by the hand of Moses and Aaron.

Our culture tends to treat religion and faith as private matters. 'What is true for you' is a catchphrase suggesting that it does not matter what you believe, as long as it works for you. Faith, though, is no more a private affair than anything else in life and, in times of trauma, we can be carried by the community of faith and the faith of the community.

The psalmist's final appeal to faith in a time of doubt is to remind himself of not only his experience of God but also the story of salvation that was told and retold countless times. These verses are a poetic revisiting of the Exodus, when Moses and Aaron led the people out of Egypt and, chased by the Egyptian armies, were made safe by the miraculous parting of the Red Sea. The origins of faith, then, are not in a rosy picture of life, but a dramatic rescue that required courage and tenacity and only succeeded as the people stayed together.

The psalmist's second response to his feelings of self-doubt is to place his experience in the perspective of both those people whom he lives among and his ancestors. Faith is not just private and it does not all depend on my believing.

Psalm 77, then, is a psalm of wisdom, penned by an ageing poet and musician who wonders if his life has been built on foundations of sand. His response is first to recall the threads of his own life experience and then to place that against the background of salvation history.

Reflection

Faith is not the feelings of the moment, nor the private beliefs of each person, but a much bigger story. Where does my own faith experience fit into the bigger picture?

MD

Profile of a prophet: Amos

Imagine that Amos the Old Testament prophet is transported by time machine from Israel in the eighth century BC to the present day. How might he feel? How would he cope?

Doubtless he would be overwhelmed by the sophisticated world in which we live. Probably he would be terrified by the many gadgets we use, staggered by the speed at which we live and startled by the noise we endure. Maybe people would laugh at the quaintness of his clothes and smile condescendingly at his general naïvety as he nervously came to terms with life in 2011.

Suppose, after a while, that he began to adapt and was no longer out of step with the culture. Would this simple farmer have anything to say to us and our world? Would he find people very different nowadays or still much the same as in his own lifetime? Would he consider our society free of the issues that plagued his own or would he see familiar sins being repeated? If he was to be invited to preach at one of our leading churches, would he use his old sermon notes?

Amos is like an uncomfortable friend who insists on telling you the truth whether you want to hear it or not. He tells it like it is. He speaks out in warning against the complacency of Israel and Judah, and their failure to match the privilege of being God's chosen people with responsible living. Corruption and injustice, exploitation and greed, hedonism and self-gratification are all exposed. Heartless faith and rigid formalism feel the lash of his tongue. No one is spared, whether royalty or religious hierarchy.

Amos is not likely to turn up at your church this Sunday, but he does have something important to say to us, because deep down nothing much has changed. Measured by the plumb line of God's unchanging standard, we find that our society has also failed to measure up. God has just as much cause to be angry with us as with Israel.

As you listen to what Amos has to say, do not expect an easy ride. He is no soothsayer. He has a message from God that challenges and rebukes. The lion still roars…

Tony Horsfall

Sunday 9 January

Amos 1:1–2 (NIV)

The lion still roars

The words of Amos, one of the shepherds of Tekoa—what he saw concerning Israel two years before the earthquake, when Uzziah was king of Judah and Jeroboam son of Jehoash was king of Israel. He said: 'The Lord roars from Zion and thunders from Jerusalem; the pastures of the shepherds dry up, and the top of Carmel withers.'

I wonder what your concept of God is. I tend to think of God as a God of love and, for that reason, I emphasise the marvellous grace of God. I find that many people, hurt and bruised by their backgrounds, greatly need to know that God loves them, he is kindly disposed towards them and wants to do them good.

I am also aware, however, that there is more to God than his unconditional love. The Bible says that God is light (1 John 1:5), meaning that he is holy and cannot compromise on sin. That means, in his love, he is not afraid to rebuke us when we do wrong and correct us when we go astray.

Keeping these twin aspects of God's character in balance is no easy matter. We tend to lean towards one or the other and are therefore in danger of having a distorted view of God. It helps to remember that God's love is always holy and his holiness is always loving. What that means is we can trust God to act in love towards us, but we must never presume on his grace or regard him as soft and sentimental: he will be as firm with us as he will be kind.

Amos brings a message of warning from God. The date is about 750BC. Although the nation has been divided—under Uzziah in the south and Jeroboam II in the north—it is a time of peace and prosperity, but also moral laxity and spiritual indifference. God is about to shake his people out of their complacency and sinful ways. The parched pasturelands tell their own story. Like a lion disturbed, God is roaring out his displeasure.

Prayer

Lord, teach us to both love and also to rightly fear you.

TH

Amos 7:14–16 (NIV)

Called by God

Amos answered Amaziah, 'I was neither a prophet nor a prophet's son, but I was a shepherd, and I also took care of sycamore-fig trees. But the Lord took me from tending the flock and said to me, "Go, prophesy to my people Israel." Now then, hear the word of the Lord.'

Amos began his ministry at the shrine of Bethel. The place, so significant in the lives of the patriarchs, had been turned into a temple of convenience under King Jeroboam I to give legitimacy to the breakaway kingdom of the north. Almost two centuries later, his namesake (Jereboam II) had installed Amaziah there as his own priest. Into that compromised situation Amos strides to declare the word of the Lord boldly.

Amos had none of the professional status of Amaziah, but he did have a call from God and that gave him his authority. He had been uprooted from his ordinary circumstances and thrust into this situation by the action of God himself. That sense of calling gave him boldness, helping him stand firm before Amaziah's powerful opposition.

Amos had no formal training either. He had not been schooled in any of the guilds of prophets popular at that time, nor mentored by any established leader. He was a simple farmer, earning a humble living from tending sheep and growing fruit. He knew God, however, and could hear his voice. He came to confront the religious establishment not with ideas of his own, but with a revelation from God.

His spiritual quality is demonstrated in the way he was obedient to his calling. His was no easy task, for his message would make him unpopular, but he was under a divine compulsion. As he declares in an earlier passage, 'The lion has roared—who will not fear? The Sovereign Lord has spoken—who can but prophesy?' (3:8)

Prophets are uncomfortable people to have around because God uses them to speak inconvenient truths. Those who pride themselves on being 'good people' hate being exposed for who they really are and readily vent their anger on the messenger. It takes great courage to declare the whole counsel of God.

Prayer

Help your servants declare your word with courage, Lord.

TH

AMOS 2:4–5 (NIV)

Judah is charged

This is what the Lord says: 'For three sins of Judah, even for four, I will not turn back my wrath. Because they have rejected the law of the Lord and have not kept his decrees, because they have been led astray by false gods, the gods their ancestors followed, I will send fire upon Judah that will consume the fortresses of Jerusalem.'

Having considered Amos the man, we turn to his message. The opening section of the book bearing his name begins with God calling the surrounding nations to account for their wrongdoing. Like a lawyer for the prosecution, the Lord lays bare the sins of their neighbours—Damascus, Gaza, and Tyre (1:3–10). Then he turns his attention to their relatives—Edom, Ammon and Moab (1:11—2:3). They have sinned repeatedly, a specific example is given and justice will be served on them.

No doubt the prophet's listeners heartily concur with this denouncement of their rivals, for it exposes the bestiality of war and man's inhumanity to man, but then comes the shock. Suddenly, Amos' attention turns to his own people. Although himself a southerner from Tekoa in Judah, he is not blind to their shortcomings or biased in their favour.

Two issues are raised. First, they have rejected the law that God gave them as an expression of their covenant relationship with him, choosing to follow their own standards and disobey his will. Second, having lost connection with the living God, they have foolishly been led into idolatry and the worship of lesser gods, repeating the mistakes of their ancestors. Having consciously and deliberately turned their backs on God time and again, discipline is inevitable. It will come in the form of enemy attack. Their defences will be breached and their fortresses set on fire. God will withhold his protection for a time, so they can taste the unpleasantness of life without him.

We must all realise that, as the apostle Paul says, God is not weak in dealing with us (2 Corinthians 13:3). Privilege brings responsibility and the Lord disciplines those he loves (Hebrews 12:5–6). He will not turn a blind eye to our sin.

Prayer

Lord, may we never excuse our sin, nor make light of it.

TH

AMOS 2:6–8 (NIV)

Israel also indicted

This is what the Lord says: 'For three sins of Israel, even for four, I will not turn back my wrath. They sell the righteous for silver, and the needy for a pair of sandals. They trample on the heads of the poor as upon the dust of the ground and deny justice to the oppressed. Father and son use the same girl and so profane my holy name. They lie down beside every altar on garments taken in pledge. In the house of their god they drink wine taken as fines.'

Although he was from Judah, Amos was called primarily to the northern kingdom, which continued to be known as Israel. Here, the prophet's attention turns unflinchingly to his hosts and the sins that contradict their relationship with God.

They are greedy for money. The reference seems to be to a corrupt judiciary where bribery is common and justice scarce. They are greedy for power. Exploitation of the poor is common and, in the stampede to get ahead, the weak are crushed. They are greedy for pleasure. The use of temple prostitutes associated with the fertility cults of Canaan has become part of the worship at Bethel. There, worshippers are intoxicated not with the Spirit but alcohol.

Altogether, this is not a very pretty picture. Notice in verse 8 that 'god' is given a small 'g' in the NIV, emphasising that the god they are worshipping is not the God Amos represents. They have turned from the living God and ended up worshipping a corrupt pagan deity. Once more, discipline is inevitable and God will act to protect his own holy name. He will act in judgment to purify his wayward people.

Money, power and sex. Are these not the gods of our age, too? It was unrestrained greed that brought chaos to the money markets of the world. Elsewhere, in some countries, powerful dictators subjugate their own people and deny them basic rights. Sexual promiscuity creates teenage pregnancies, sexually transmitted diseases, broken families and fatherless children. Binge drinking blights our cities. Are we more sophisticated than eighth-century Israel? Certainly. Are we morally more advanced? Certainly not.

Prayer

Lord, forgive our nations for drifting away from you.

TH

AMOS 3:1–4 (NIV)

Privilege and responsibility

Hear this word the Lord has spoken against you, O people of Israel—against the whole family I brought up out of Egypt: 'You only have I chosen of all the families of the earth; therefore I will punish you for all your sins.' Do two walk together unless they have agreed to do so? Does a lion roar in the thicket when he has no prey? Does he growl in his den when he has caught nothing?

Amos speaks to the whole of Israel now, northern and southern kingdoms combined, reminding them of their spiritual history and the enormous privilege of being God's chosen people.

The exodus from Egypt was one of the most significant events in Israel's past, demonstrating the power of God in delivering his people from slavery. Not only that, but God also guided them through the wilderness, defeated their enemies and brought them into the promised land—facts Amos is keen to remind his hearers about (see also 2:9–10). Such acts of grace and power should have created within them a strong sense of identity and gratitude. Instead, Israel has forgotten her true identity and become detached from her redeemer.

It is a spiritual principle that privilege brings responsibility: 'From everyone who has been given much, much will be demanded; and from the one who has been entrusted with much, much more will be asked' (Luke 12:48). Israel's failure to live up to her high calling will mean painful discipline until she repents and returns to the Lord.

It should be pointed out that God's only purpose in discipline is restoration. He is not lashing out in frustration or throwing a tantrum in rage. He desires agreement—the kind of harmony where fellowship is restored between him and his people and where, once again, they live to demonstrate his love and express his life to the surrounding nations. This had always been his purpose for Israel and nothing has changed.

As we reflect on the blessing of God in our own lives, we must beware taking it for granted or failing to live up to our calling to be lights in this dark world.

Reflection

'Great gifts mean great responsibilities' (Luke 12:48, THE MESSAGE).

TH

Amos 4:6–9 (NIV, abridged)

Refusal to return

'I gave you empty stomachs in every city and lack of bread in every town, yet you have not returned to me,' declares the Lord. 'I also withheld rain from you when the harvest was still three months away. I sent rain on one town, but withheld it from another... People staggered from town to town for water but did not get enough to drink, yet you have not returned to me,' declares the Lord. 'Many times I struck your gardens and vineyards... with blight and mildew. Locusts devoured your fig and olive trees, yet you have not returned to me,' declares the Lord.

Amos is very specific in terms of the way in which he says God will discipline his people. The fourth chapter reads like a sermon that he might have preached on the subject and, in verses 6–11, he identifies five current realities that reflect the hand of God—famine, drought, crop failure, disease and defeat. One or two of these might be chance events, but the combination of unfortunate occurrences suggests to Amos that God is speaking to his people through them. As C.S. Lewis put it in *The Problem of Pain* (1940), 'God whispers to us in our pleasures, speaks to us in our conscience, but shouts in our pain: it is His megaphone to rouse a deaf world.'

In a society that has relegated God to the sidelines, the idea that he might be speaking to us in our misfortunes seems strange. We have accustomed ourselves to coping with what life throws at us, adjusting as best we can and moving forwards again. Seldom do we stop and ask the question, 'What might God be saying to me in this?'

Israel's response was much the same. In today's reading, the issue is drought: some parts of the country have rain, others mysteriously do not. Water is one of the most precious commodities and we soon suffer without it, but no one stops to ask, 'Why is this happening to us?' Amos alone interprets the gracious discipline of God in the weather patterns.

We catch something of the deep disappointment of God in the oft-repeated words, 'yet you have not returned to me'. The lover is spurned. The rebels dig their heels in. Resistance continues.

Prayer

Lord, forgive our foolish ways.

TH

Saturday 15 January

Amos 5:4–6 (NIV)

The divine remedy

> This is what the Lord says to the house of Israel: 'Seek me and live; do not seek Bethel, do not go to Gilgal, do not journey to Beersheba. For Gilgal will surely go into exile, and Bethel will be reduced to nothing.' Seek the Lord and live, or he will sweep through the house of Joseph like a fire; it will devour, and Bethel will have no one to quench it.

Pilgrimage seems to have been a common expression of religious life at the time of Amos, with three particular shrines deemed the most popular—Bethel, Beersheba and Gilgal. Each had played a significant part in Israel's spiritual history, so, in one sense, it is not surprising that people wanted to see these sacred places, to walk where the patriarchs had walked (Bethel and Beersheba), to stand where Joshua had stood (Gilgal).

Pilgrimage, however, can have little meaning if it is not connected with seeking God and that is what appears to be the bone of contention as far as Amos is concerned. Indeed, some of these religious shrines had so lost their way that they promoted sinfulness rather than holiness (4:4) and were best avoided.

The answer to Israel's plight is to seek God afresh, from their hearts, in humble repentance and renewed surrender. It is an internal journey that is required, a journey of the heart, not a trek across country. God can be found wherever we are if we care to search for him in sincerity and truth.

There are two lessons that we can learn from this passage. First, even churches with a good reputation can lose their way unless they continually encourage people to seek God for themselves. Past history is no guarantee of divine presence today. Second, it is always easier to go somewhere and do something than to turn inwards and discover the reality of God within our own hearts. We can all substitute various kinds of activism for the reality of knowing God in a deep and personal way, but only when we truly seek God will we truly live.

Prayer

Cause me, Lord, to seek for you with all my heart.
Reveal yourself to me afresh.

TH

Sunday 16 January

Amos 5:14–15 (NIV)

The divine desire

> Seek good, not evil, that you may live. Then the Lord God Almighty will be with you, just as you say he is. Hate evil, love good; maintain justice in the courts. Perhaps the Lord God Almighty will have mercy on the remnant of Joseph.

If God's remedy for his people is that they should seek him afresh, his desire is that their lives should then reflect more fully the fact that they know him and are in relationship with him. Knowing God is not simply a matter of personal piety. It is about how we live and, in particular, how we treat other people. We are called to love God and also to love our neighbour. There is a social dimension to true faith.

The first step towards such true faith is to seek God. The second step is to seek good—good in the sense of doing what is right and expressing the mercy and compassion of God in all our interactions with others and working energetically for the benefit of those less fortunate. This is neither lofty idealism nor sympathetic daydreaming. Neither is it the latest cause of the political activist, nor the newest project of the humanist. It is the passionate expression of the heart of a caring God through the hands and feet of his willing people.

For Amos and the other prophets, true religion is always authenticated by this external expression. Micah sums it up beautifully: 'He has showed you, O man, what is good. And what does the Lord require of you? To act justly and to love mercy and to walk humbly with your God' (6:8).

Such compassionate living must find its spring of life in God. We are to seek God first and then do good afterwards. In this way, we can sustain our involvement in the world and, at the same time, give glory to God.

The disease of our consumer society has been described as 'affluenza' and its symptoms are self-centred interest and material gain. Only God can move us from such a narrow focus and enlarge our hearts to meet the needs of others.

Prayer

Lord, show me how I can be involved. Release me from my selfish ways.

TH

True religion

'I hate, I despise your religious feasts; I cannot stand your assemblies. Even though you bring me burnt offerings and grain offerings, I will not accept them. Though you bring choice fellowship offerings, I will have no regard for them. Away with the noise of your songs! I will not listen to the music of your harps. But let justice roll on like a river, righteousness like a never-failing stream!'

The theme of practical religion continues in this section. For Amos, true worship takes place outside the sanctuary as well as inside. Indeed, unless there is an external application of our faith, it is worthless. As the apostle James said, faith without works is dead (2:17).

There is no doubt that the shrines of Bethel, Beersheba and Gilgal were doing a roaring trade and, outwardly, appeared to be successful. There were feast days and festivals, offerings and sacrifices, quality music and hearty singing. People loved to attend and they had a good time. The only problem was, God was not pleased! He hated these gatherings, would not accept the offerings and did not listen to the worship songs. Why? Because it was all detached from reality. There was no compassionate outworking of the pious words in the lives of the people.

True religion starts with righteousness—that is, by being in a right relationship with God. How is that achieved? Simply by believing God, as Abraham did (Genesis 15:6; Galatians 3:6). Such a faith is not passive, however, but expressed externally by doing what is right—and that is what justice is. It means acting in all situations with honesty, integrity, fairness and compassion, so that the stream of righteousness—which has its source in God and is internal and spiritual—flows outwards into a river of justice—which is external and practical. Because the source of our righteousness never dries up, the river of compassionate caring never stops either.

What does God think about the worship in your church? What does he think about your faith? Take a moment to review how what you believe affects the way you live.

Prayer

Help me to express my love for you, Lord, in love of others.

TH

Tuesday 18 January

AMOS 7:1–3 (NIV)

A prophet's intercession

> This is what the Sovereign Lord showed me: he was preparing swarms of locusts after the king's share had been harvested and just as the second crop was coming up. When they had stripped the land clean, I cried out, 'Sovereign Lord, forgive! How can Jacob survive? He is so small!' So the Lord relented. 'This will not happen,' the Lord said.

Amos, as we have seen, is a straight-talking person who gets right to the point and does not mince his words. He analyses the situation objectively and expresses clearly and directly what he hears God say. This is the way of the prophet. Amos is not without heart, though, and he loves his own people, he longs for their renewal.

In the first of four visions, Amos is shown by God, in a pictorial way, the true state of the nation and it is a frightening picture. Locusts were a constant plague and nuisance to farmers at that time and an obvious symbol of the judgment that was to come. Moved by what he sees and understands in his spirit, Amos calls out to the Lord in anguished intercession on behalf of his people.

Intercession is an important ministry of the Church. We are called to 'pray in the Spirit on all occasions with all kinds of prayers and requests' (Ephesians 6:18). It is a heartfelt cry that comes from deep within, an expression of yearning and longing that God will hear.

Does prayer make a difference? Most certainly it does. Amos asks for forgiveness and pleads for mercy on behalf of Israel and God hears his prayer. God relents and the threatened catastrophe does not happen. Although the people deserve to be punished, they are spared, for now at least, because of the impassioned plea of the prophet. Prayer can change history and, although there is great mystery here, it is the means by which God brings about his purposes.

If prayer makes such a difference, then, why is there so little prayer in the average church outside the weekly Sunday services? Why is the prayer meeting (if there is one) often the most poorly attended of all church events?

Prayer

Lord, teach us to pray.

TH

Wednesday 19 January

Amos7:7–9 (NIV)

A prophet's understanding

> This is what he showed me: the Lord was standing by a wall that had been built true to plumb, with a plumb line in his hand. And the Lord asked me, 'What do you see, Amos?' 'A plumb line,' I replied. Then the Lord said, 'Look, I am setting a plumb line among my people Israel; I will spare them no longer. The high places of Isaac will be destroyed and the sanctuaries of Israel will be ruined; with my sword I will rise against the house of Jeroboam.'

A plumb line is a simple but accurate tool used by builders to determine whether or not something is perfectly vertical—in other words, upright. Used since ancient times, it consists of a string with a weight attached, which, when suspended and allowed to come to rest, shows if a wall is straight.

The third of the visions in this chapter, it gives Amos an insight into how God is 'measuring' his people. When the nation came into being, it was like a wall that had been built straight and true by a master builder, but what about now? Has the wall begun to lean over? Is it in danger of falling down? The implication is that Israel is no longer upright but ready to collapse.

The objective standard that God uses to test his people is, of course, his law, given to Israel at Mount Sinai and distilled in the Ten Commandments (Exodus 20:1–17). Against this unchanging line of obedience to God's revealed will, everything and everyone is measured—popular religious practice, professional priests, the nation's king, leaders and people—and the verdict is that they are no longer 'upright'.

We all have many ways of assessing how we are doing. Often we compare ourselves to other people, feeling justified because we are not as bad as they are, or use some lesser standard, contenting ourselves with the thought that 'everybody does it so it cannot be wrong'. Some wish to move away from absolute standards altogether. Thus we quiet our conscience and fail to register our own crookedness.

God, however, is unchanging in his requirements. His measurement is the only one that counts and is the one to which we must align.

Prayer

Lord, keep me standing straight and true.

TH

Thursday 20 January

AMOS 8:11–12 (NIV)

Famine of a different kind

> 'The days are coming,' declares the Sovereign Lord, 'when I will send a famine through the land—not a famine of food or a thirst for water, but a famine of hearing the words of the Lord. Men will stagger from sea to sea and wander from north to east, searching for the word of the Lord, but they will not find it.'

So far, the disciplines of God have been of a physical nature, but now we see a threat of a spiritual character—the withdrawal of the 'words of the Lord'. He has been speaking to his people clearly and consistently, but no one is listening. If this unresponsiveness continues, he is saying, he will stop speaking altogether. The word of the Lord will become as scarce as bread in a famine. Prophets like Amos will have no revelation to bring, no further word of warning or entreaty.

To understand the seriousness of this impending situation, remember the words of Jesus: 'It is written, "Man does not live on bread alone, but on every word that comes from the mouth of God"' (Matthew 4:4, from Deuteronomy 8:3). This quotation refers to the gift of manna and its spiritual lesson. Just as bread is vital for the body's needs, so the word of God is vital for the needs of the soul. We are spiritual as well as physical beings, so if we neglect to care for our souls, we suffer as a result.

The word of God provides us with wisdom and understanding for daily living. It reveals to us the will of God and shows us the way of salvation. It contains encouragement and reassurances and its promises give us confidence and hope. It teaches us the truth and points us in the right direction.

It is easy to take common things, like bread, for granted. It is shameful to think that we might take for granted the fact that God can and will speak to us regularly and consistently through his word. Do we value this blessing? When God does speak to us, whether personally or corporately, do we treasure his words and act on them?

Prayer

Thank you for speaking, Lord. Give me ears to hear.

TH

A prophet's revelation

'In that day I will restore David's fallen tent. I will repair its broken places, restore its ruins, and build it as it used to be, so that they may possess the remnant of Edom and all the nations that bear my name,' declares the Lord, who will do these things.

Thankfully, the prophecy of Amos is not all doom and gloom. Even this most serious of prophets is allowed to glimpse the wonderful future that ultimately awaits the people of God. His work is not just to 'forth-tell' (spelling out divine displeasure), but also to foretell (describing a glorious restoration).

This message of hope looks beyond the disciplinary time of the exile to the period when Israel will return to her land and, once again, be in tune with God in a way similar to that experienced during the golden age of the reign of King David. We can see the fulfilment in the return from exile that took place under the leadership of Ezra and Nehemiah, with the rebuilding of the city of Jerusalem, the restoration of worship and life once more being organised under the rule of God.

Amos' words here have a much greater significance, however. They reach beyond even that period to the age of the Church and, indeed, to the expansion of the Church worldwide. That is certainly how James, the leader of the Jerusalem church, understood it (in Acts 15:13–18, he quotes this passage). As the early Church began to grow and expand and the Gentiles started to believe as well, the first believers were taken by surprise. James helps his fellow believers to understand that is exactly what Amos had predicted—the growth of the kingdom of God throughout the entire world.

The purpose of God—to bless Israel and, through her, to bless the nations—is a purpose that cannot be thwarted. Even the disobedience and waywardness of his people cannot prevent it from happening. The Church will grow and the kingdom will come; nothing can stop it. God himself will bring this about, so we must not be discouraged by what we may see about us today.

Prayer

Lord, let your kingdom come!

TH

AMOS 9:13–15 (NIV)

A prophet's expectation

> 'The days are coming,' declares the Lord, 'when the reaper will be overtaken by the ploughman and the planter by the one treading grapes. New wine will drip from the mountains and flow from all the hills. I will bring back my exiled people Israel; they will rebuild the ruined cities and live in them. They will plant vineyards and drink their wine; they will make gardens and eat their fruit. I will plant Israel in their own land, never again to be uprooted from the land I have given them,' says the Lord your God.

The theme of restoration continues with a beautiful description of life under the rule of God. It may be a somewhat idealised portrayal of what life could be like once again, and there is clearly some poetic licence here, but, in later years, it must have given a wonderful sense of hope and longing to the people that God would never let go of them. Even if exiled in judgment, they would return under his mercy.

Beyond that, the passage can be read as speaking figuratively in harvest terms of the expansion of the Church, giving hope of revival and restoration, of 'times of refreshing' coming from the hand of the Lord (Acts 3:19). Those who have experienced such times often speak of the sense of 'heaven on earth' that accompanies a movement of the Spirit—and 'reaping' is a common biblical metaphor for effective evangelism.

Yet, for us, these words are probably best interpreted in terms of the reign of Christ on earth following his return. Then, nature will itself be set free from its bondage and the earth will be restored to the wonder and beauty of Eden. Released from the curse of the Fall, the created order will display its true glory. Peace and harmony will flood the world. Redemption's work will have been completed, the kingdom will have come on earth again, and the king will be among his people.

However bleak the world feels some days, this is our hope, too.

Prayer

Lord, when darkness seems to rule the day, remind us of this,
our sure and certain hope.

TH

Holy fire

These readings on 'holy fire' fall during one of the coldest, darkest times of year—if you live in the northern hemisphere, that is. The festive atmosphere of Christmas has faded away, even if we have kept the decorations up until Epiphany. While your personal January may be cheered by a birthday or similar celebration, it can feel like a long and weary progression of days until the first hint of spring.

If we are used to the wall-to-wall warmth of central heating and the ease of flicking a switch to flood a room with light, it can be hard to appreciate the importance of a fire on a cold morning or a candle on a dark night. My family and I sometimes stay at a cottage where there is no heat until you kindle the woodstove and the limited electricity supply comes from a small wind generator. After a day or so, both light and heat are appreciated as the precious resources that they really are.

We should remember that when we read Bible passages about 'light', the words were written many centuries before the invention of electric light. That means, as far as the original audience was concerned (and for generations after), 'light' and 'fire' came to the same thing—a living flame, whether an oil lamp, a manageable blaze on a hearth or a catastrophic inferno.

Over the next two weeks, we will reflect on passages from across scripture to do with fire and light to see what they can teach us about our faith and God. We will ponder the manifestation of the Lord as mysterious fire in the desert and the Holy Spirit appearing as flame and wind at Pentecost. We will think about how fire is presented as both purifying and destructive and wrestle with the implications of the 'fires of judgment'.

Along the way, we will consider two special days in the Church calendar, both of which have associations with light and fire—Candlemas (also known as the Presentation of Christ in the Temple), which falls on 2 February, and 1 February, when we remember Brigid of Kildare.

Naomi Starkey

Ezekiel 1:4–5, 22, 26–28 (NRSV, abridged)

Something like

As I looked, a stormy wind came out of the north: a great cloud with brightness around it and fire flashing forth continually... In the middle of it was something like four living creatures... Over the heads of the living creatures there was something like a dome, shining like crystal... And above the dome over their heads there was something like a throne, in appearance like sapphire; and seated above the likeness of a throne was something that seemed like a human form. Upward from what appeared like the loins I saw something like gleaming amber, something that looked like fire enclosed all round... This was the appearance of the likeness of the glory of the Lord.

This astonishing vision is probably less well-known than Isaiah's experience (see later this week), but it is an equally bold attempt to express the inexpressible. Do take a moment at some point to read the whole chapter and imagine your response if a friend or relative returned from a stroll by the river with such a tale to tell!

We do not have space to explore the possible significance of the four living creatures, the crystal dome, the sapphire throne and so on. What we can appreciate here, though, is the dazzling poetic imagery and the way it establishes the theme of God's sovereignty, which pervades the book of Ezekiel. There are representations of many kinds of animal, all-seeing eyes, the mention of a rainbow, that ancient symbol of hope, and God enthroned above all.

Ezekiel's vision came while he was among the Jewish exiles in Babylon and unequivocally demonstrates that the Lord is God of the entire cosmos. The chosen people are far from the temple, but not far from God—and the power of the Almighty is not in any way diminished by a foreign context. Although the tremendous glory of the Lord is heightened by contrasting it with the people's sinfulness, Ezekiel's message is ultimately one of hope and restoration and the unstoppable power of heaven.

Reflection

Note how the prophet carefully states that 'this was the appearance of the likeness of the glory of the Lord', rather than declaring boldly 'I saw God'. Let's maintain a similar humility when we share our experiences of God with others.

NS

EXODUS 13:20–22 (NRSV)

Fire in the wilderness

[The Israelites] set out from Succoth, and camped at Etham, on the edge of the wilderness. The Lord went in front of them in a pillar of cloud by day, to lead them along the way, and in a pillar of fire by night, to give them light, so that they might travel by day and by night. Neither the pillar of cloud by day nor the pillar of fire by night left its place in front of the people.

The phrase 'a pillar of cloud' conjures up images of a tornado—that fearful twisting spiral reaching down from thunderous clouds to wreak havoc where it touches down. This cloud, however, was a guiding presence, a way of indicating a path through pathless places, and, at night, perhaps its fiery appearance was warming and protective for the people as well.

Anybody who has ever camped in the wild will know how comforting a fire can be, even if they are not camping in a place where there are predators large and fierce enough to fancy them for a midnight snack. Firelight means companionship, a measure of comfort and the possibility of food. Mountaineer Joe Simpson's book *Touching the Void* (Vintage, 1988) describes his agonising solitary journey to safety after a terrible fall and tells of his anguish at crawling, after nightfall, over the final ridge before base camp—only to see no sign of light beyond. For a desolate few hours, he assumed that his companions had given up hope and left him (fortunately, they had not).

Whatever our favoured brand of churchmanship, we can gain solace and inspiration from physical reminders of God's protecting and consoling presence in our places of worship, whether in the form of a simple cross, a beautifully painted icon or the sanctuary light burning to indicate that the reserved sacrament is housed nearby. We may feel that it is preferable to believe in our hearts that God is with us and that he loves us, but sometimes even superheroes of faith can benefit from an outward sign of otherwise intangible grace.

Reflection

'The Lord is your keeper; the Lord is your shade at your right hand. The sun shall not strike you by day, nor the moon by night' (Psalm 121:5–6).

NS

2 KINGS 2:9–12 (NRSV)

Chariot of fire

> When they had crossed [the Jordan], Elijah said to Elisha, 'Tell me what I may do for you, before I am taken from you.' Elisha said, 'Please let me inherit a double share of your spirit.' He responded, 'You have asked a hard thing; yet, if you see me as I am being taken from you, it will be granted you; if not, it will not.' As they continued walking and talking, a chariot of fire and horses of fire separated the two of them, and Elijah ascended in a whirlwind into heaven. Elisha kept watching and crying out, 'Father, father! The chariots of Israel and its horsemen!' But when he could no longer see him, he grasped his own clothes and tore them in two pieces.

What a way to go! Probably not most people's choice when envisaging their preferred death, though. It sounds like an episode from the TV series *Lost*, where plane crash survivors on a remote island contend with an increasingly bizarre plotline involving time travel, monsters and mysticism. I wonder how Elijah felt as he made that final, dizzying ascent? Would he have been terrified or exhilarated by the astonishing light?

Another example of somebody being 'taken' by God is Enoch (Genesis 5:21–24). Hebrews 11:5 explains that this happened because he had 'pleased God' and cites him as a hero of salvation history. Similarly, Elijah's end befits his enduring status in both Jewish and Christian thought. Indeed, traditionally, an empty seat is still kept at the Passover table in case he returns.

Although forewarned that his master was leaving (and despite the divine honour implicit in the manner of his leaving), Elisha is distraught. Commentators cannot agree on the meaning of his incoherent cry as he watches, but he shows his sorrow by tearing his clothes. Even the hope of the promised 'double portion' of Elijah's prophetic gift does not stop him grieving. Envisaging our loved ones in the glory of the Lord's presence does not stop us longing for them to be with us again. That is not wrong; it is simply human.

Reflection

Elijah experienced God as both heavenly fire and a gentle whisper.
Let us be open to however God chooses to reveal himself to us.

NS

Wednesday 26 January

EXODUS 3:1–5 (NRSV)

This great sight

Moses was keeping the flock of his father-in-law Jethro, the priest of Midian; he led his flock beyond the wilderness, and came to Horeb, the mountain of God. There the angel of the Lord appeared to him in a flame of fire out of a bush; he looked, and the bush was blazing, yet it was not consumed. Then Moses said, 'I must turn aside and look at this great sight, and see why the bush is not burned up.' When the Lord saw that he had turned aside to see, God called to him out of the bush, 'Moses, Moses!' And he said, 'Here I am.' Then he said, 'Come no closer! Remove the sandals from your feet, for the place on which you are standing is holy ground.'

This divine encounter is no huge storm of light and fire, but a phenomenon intriguing enough to catch Moses' attention. What if he had ignored it? God's sovereign purposes would not have been thwarted by a man too lacking in curiosity or scared to draw close, but subsequent events may have unfolded differently.

Are we inclined always to hurry on by and never 'turn aside'? Although life is often unavoidably busy, we may risk missing a transformative encounter more often than we know.

Moses was a fugitive, washed up in the wilderness because he had tried to act the hero and use his adoptive Egyptian status to save a fellow Hebrew but ended up a murderer instead (Exodus 2:11–15). Now, because he is prepared to 'turn aside', his circumstances are turned upside down. The God of his true fathers, Abraham, Isaac and Jacob (3:6), the God who has done great things in the past, will act again.

God's calling to Moses proved to be an extraordinarily difficult one, bringing suffering not only to himself but also his wider family. Sometimes he must have recalled this desert encounter as a reminder that his life was not his own—he had given himself in obedience to the Lord Almighty.

Reflection

Moses had to remove his shoes because he was on holy ground, standing in God's presence. Followers of a number of world faiths still do the same before worship; how should Christians acknowledge God's presence?

NS

Thursday 27 January

ISAIAH 6:1, 4–7 (NRSV)

The splendour of his majesty

> In the year that King Uzziah died, I saw the Lord sitting on a throne, high and lofty; and the hem of his robe filled the temple... The pivots on the thresholds shook at the voices of [the seraphs] who called, and the house filled with smoke. And I said: 'Woe is me! I am lost, for I am a man of unclean lips, and I live among a people of unclean lips; yet my eyes have seen the King, the Lord of hosts!' Then one of the seraphs flew to me, holding a live coal that had been taken from the altar with a pair of tongs. The seraph touched my mouth with it and said: 'Now that this has touched your lips, your guilt has departed and your sin is blotted out.'

This prophetic calling is one of the best-known in scripture. It shares many similarities with Ezekiel's experience and descriptions in the book of Revelation (4:3–11, for example). A modern-day writer attempting to express what was seen and heard might perhaps use strobe lighting, throbbing bass guitar lines and hallucinogenic colours.

In this passage, we find the theme of purging fire, something we will consider in later readings. For now, we will focus on Isaiah's response to finding himself surrounded by the light of heaven. He does not need to be told that he is 'unclean'—in the presence of the Lord of hosts, he knows that he is as unworthy of love and mercy as the most cynical and sinful of the people. The brighter the light, the clearer we see the grime and flaws, whether in our surroundings or in ourselves.

Reassuringly, no sooner has Isaiah acknowledged his guilt than the coal plucked from the altar burns away his guilt. The seraph, servant of God, tells him that his sin is not only forgiven but also 'blotted out', utterly cleansed. The prophet is now prepared to serve the Lord.

Reflection

Imagine yourself in the shadowless brightness of God's gaze.
Is there anything that you would rather keep hidden? Realise the futility of such a hope and ask for mercy, knowing that God is more than willing to grant it.

NS

Acts 2:1–4 (NRSV)

Blazing Spirit

When the day of Pentecost had come, they were all together in one place. And suddenly from heaven there came a sound like the rush of a violent wind, and it filled the entire house where they were sitting. Divided tongues, as of fire, appeared among them, and a tongue rested on each of them. All of them were filled with the Holy Spirit and began to speak in other languages, as the Spirit gave them ability.

Pentecost fell on the 50th day after the sabbath of Passover week, originally celebrated as the harvest festival and later linked to commemorating the giving of the Law on Sinai. A highly symbolic occasion, then, for this dramatic moment of wind and fire that took place seven weeks after Jesus' death and ten days after his ascension, as the pattern of the Christian calendar still reminds us.

'They', referred to in the passage, were not just the eleven remaining apostles (following the loss of Judas) plus their new recruit, Matthias, but the wider circle of Jesus' followers. This group had continued to meet together, waiting and hoping for the coming of the Spirit that their Master had promised before his bodily presence left them (Acts 1:8). Now, at Pentecost, that promise would be fulfilled and the next phase in the spreading of the gospel message would begin. The harvest would ultimately be global, but also personally costly for many of those gathered in that house.

The small tongues of flame were a sign of God's presence coming to indwell each one of the disciples. It was not so much that everyone had their own personal 'bit of God', but they were drawn into the one great blaze of the Spirit. All had been cleansed from sin, for ever, through Jesus' atoning death, so all could be drawn into the Spirit's work of testifying to what God had done through his Son.

Reflection

The gift of 'other languages' (here meaning other human languages, not glossolalia, *also known as 'speaking in tongues') was bestowed for a specific and weighty purpose. Jesus' followers were to share the good news with the crowds gathered in the city, rather than stay indoors and enjoy a private worship session.*

NS

MALACHI 3:1–4 (NRSV, ABRIDGED)

Refiner's fire

> See, I am sending my messenger to prepare the way before me, and the Lord whom you seek will suddenly come to his temple... But who can endure the day of his coming, and who can stand when he appears? For he is like a refiner's fire and like fullers' soap; he will sit as a refiner and purifier of silver, and he will purify the descendants of Levi and refine them like gold and silver, until they present offerings to the Lord in righteousness. Then the offering of Judah and Jerusalem will be pleasing to the Lord as in the days of old and as in former years.

As well as offering warmth and light, as well as being beautiful and at times terrifying to behold, fire can be used to cleanse. Our passage today speaks of 'the day of his coming'—the 'day of the Lord' mentioned again and again in the scriptures as the time when God will come in power to right every wrong. Even the 'descendants of Levi', the priestly tribe, are not exempt from the refiner's fire—leaders, as well as the people, must be made clean in order to be 'pleasing to the Lord'.

The refining imagery here is linked to two industrial processes—washing woollen cloth and heating metal to remove impurities. In both processes, the result is a useful and valuable product—one made fit for purpose. One of the key innovations of 19th-century Britain was the Bessemer process, enabling the mass-production of malleable steel from a brittle form of iron and so vastly expanding the scope of the Industrial Revolution.

Such processes always involve stress, hard work and the expenditure of physical and mental energy. They are not easy, but the end result is worth it. Our tendency is to assume that, 'if it hurts, it must be bad for us', yet God does not apply the 'refiner's fire' or 'fullers' soap' for sadistic ends. What he does need to do, though, is cleanse and shape his children so that they are readied for his holy and eternal purposes.

Reflection

Dare we ask God to refine us and refine our churches
until we are fit for purpose?

NS

Sunday 30 January

MATTHEW 3:10–12 (NRSV)

Burned clean

'Even now the axe is lying at the root of the trees; every tree therefore that does not bear good fruit is cut down and thrown into the fire. I baptise you with water for repentance, but one who is more powerful than I is coming after me; I am not worthy to carry his sandals. He will baptise you with the Holy Spirit and fire. His winnowing-fork is in his hand, and he will clear his threshing-floor and will gather his wheat into the granary; but the chaff he will burn with unquenchable fire.'

These verses come from one of John the Baptist's famously fiery speeches. Addressing two of the leading faith groups of the day, which had come for baptism (v. 7), he denounces them as a 'brood of vipers' and adds for good measure that God could create children of the Covenant from the stones underfoot (v. 9). Despite their social status, the religious leaders are far from beyond reproach. John then describes the one 'coming after' him, who will bring a new baptism of Spirit and fire. To explain what he will be like, he evokes a farmer hard at work, flexing his muscles to swing his axe and clear the dead wood, sifting straw from grain and burning the waste until not a trace is left.

We may find these words uncomfortable because we struggle to relate them to ourselves or to those we know and love. Should we be trembling lest the celestial farmer judge us (or them) as useless and throw us into the unquenchable fire like a pile of old sticks?

It is important to remember that the burning branches are not being punished; they are being tidied away, as today we shred and compost garden waste. The farmer is making the field fit for purpose (an echo of yesterday's reflection). Rather than worrying that we might be 'dead wood', we should reflect on the 'chaff' in our lives that needs to be discarded—the wrong attitudes, unhelpful habits and the cobwebbed corners that we hide from God's love and grace.

Reflection

'I am the vine, you are the branches. Those who abide in me and I in them bear much fruit, because apart from me you can do nothing' (John 15:5).

NS

REVELATION 20:11–15 (NRSV, ABRIDGED)

Lake of fire

> Then I saw a great white throne and the one who sat on it; the earth and heaven fled from his presence... And I saw the dead, great and small, standing before the throne, and books were opened. Also another book was opened, the book of life. And the dead were judged according to their works, as recorded in the books... Then Death and Hades were thrown into the lake of fire. This is the second death, the lake of fire; and anyone whose name was not found written in the book of life was thrown into the lake of fire.

This is one of those passages over which people have argued for centuries, so we cannot hope to tie up the loose ends on this single page! That said, there are two issues to bear in mind. First, Revelation should not be read in a woodenly literalistic way—it is an apocalypse, a dramatic genre, using vivid imagery to present spiritual truths. A good commentary or well-trained preacher is an essential aid to understanding it.

Second, we should not confuse these verses with verses 9–10, where the hellish enemies of God are 'tormented day and night forever and ever' in the fiery lake. According to one well-respected view, our passage for today indicates that, while eternal life is the reward of the faithful, the rest are simply annihilated, ceasing to exist for ever, in a 'second death'. Note, too, that the dead are judged 'according to their works', rather than according to their faith. Perhaps (whisper it) God cares more about how we lead our lives than the correctness of our doctrine.

As we reflect on these huge matters, we must hold on to what scripture tells us—that God loves the world so much, he sent his one and only Son to save every single one of us. Salvation is a gift freely available to all who choose to receive it.

Reflection

To have a hell of torment, with no remission or hope of repentance, is to have God sustaining, in his perfect new creation, a part of it which will always be in rebellion against him, and which can only be described as evil.

Marcus Maxwell, *Revelation* (BRF, 2005), p.195

NS

LEVITICUS 6:8–10, 13 (NRSV, ABRIDGED)

Perpetual fire

The Lord spoke to Moses, saying: Command Aaron and his sons, saying: This is the ritual of the burnt-offering. The burnt-offering itself shall remain on the hearth upon the altar all night until the morning, while the fire on the altar shall be kept burning. The priest shall put on his linen vestments... and he shall take up the ashes to which the fire has reduced the burnt-offering on the altar, and place them beside the altar... A perpetual fire shall be kept burning on the altar; it shall not go out.

Today the Church calendar commemorates Brigid of Kildare (c. 454–525), renowned for establishing religious communities in Ireland after being inspired by Patrick's preaching. The most famous of these communities was for both men and women at Kildare and offered hospitality, education and worship. Stories tell that her pagan father named Brigid after the Celtic fire goddess and, interestingly, when she came to Kildare, she decided to maintain the ancient, pre-Christian 'perpetual fire' there, choosing to 'rebrand' it as the light of Christ. That fire may have burned right up to the 16th-century suppression of the monasteries, but was then not rekindled until 1993. It is now tended by the Brigidine Sisters, a restoration of Brigid's original monastic order.

Brigid's reinterpretation of the pagan fire as Christian was an approach, in many ways, typical of Celtic spirituality. Instead of labouring to remove every vestige of the old ways, the tendency has been to absorb and redirect the best of them into a Christian worldview. Thus, people came to realise that the beliefs and powers they held as sacred were not, in themselves, evil but merely inadequate—just a vague intimation of the true Lord of creation.

It is interesting to realise how a 'perpetual fire' was part of the worship ritual ordained by God for the Israelites. The fire of sacrifice purified the people by consuming the offerings that they brought to symbolise their sin, so its continuing to burn was a powerful sign that God's purifying work never comes to an end.

Reflection

What are the 'old ways' of our culture that we can redirect so that they honour the Lord God?

NS

Luke 2:25–32 (NRSV, abridged)

The light of the world

> Now there was a man in Jerusalem whose name was Simeon; this man was righteous and devout... and the Holy Spirit rested on him. It had been revealed to him by the Holy Spirit that he would not see death before he had seen the Lord's Messiah. Guided by the Spirit, Simeon came into the temple; and when the parents brought in the child Jesus... Simeon took him in his arms and praised God, saying: 'Master, now you are dismissing your servant in peace, according to your word; for my eyes have seen your salvation, which you have prepared in the presence of all peoples, a light for revelation to the Gentiles and for glory to your people Israel.'

Today, the Church remembers Jesus' parents bringing him to the temple to be 'presented to the Lord' as the Law prescribed for a firstborn male (v. 23) and for Mary's ritual purification, 40 days after the birth. Those relatively routine events were, however, an occasion for yet another reminder of Jesus' extraordinary destiny. Not only was there the prophetic meeting with Simeon, but an elderly woman, the prophet Anna, also approached and proclaimed the baby as a sign of hope 'to all who were looking for the redemption of Jerusalem' (v. 38).

This day is also known as Candlemas because it is traditionally when church candles for use over the coming year are blessed. In pre-Christian times, a festival of light took place at this time, marking the midpoint between the shortest day and the spring equinox (and so the midpoint of winter). What better way to redeem this ancient and understandable impulse than to link it to remembering the Christ-light breaking into the world?

Candlemas marks a turning point in the Church calendar, when the focus shifts from 'after Christmas' to 'before Easter'. The words that Simeon goes on to speak to Mary are soberingly prescient: her child will be 'a sign that will be opposed' and, ominously, her own soul will be pierced as with a sword (vv. 34–35). The brighter the light, the sharper the shadows.

Reflection

'The light shines in the darkness, and the darkness did not overcome it' (John 1:5).

NS

Thursday 3 February

Luke 8:16–18 (NRSV)

Letting the light shine

> [Jesus said] 'No one after lighting a lamp hides it under a jar, or puts it under a bed, but puts it on a lampstand, so that those who enter may see the light. Nor nothing is hidden that will not be disclosed, nor is anything secret that will not become known and come to light. Then pay attention to how you listen; for to those who have, more will be given; and from those who do not have, even what they seem to have will be taken away.'

In the introduction to these readings I mentioned how a few days away from the National Grid is a good reminder of the value of light. There is effort involved in pouring out lamp oil, trimming a wick, ensuring protection from draughts and—as Jesus humorously points out—you do not go to all that trouble only to hide the light under a bed.

The point of light (obviously) is to provide illumination, not only for ourselves but also for those who enter the lit room. Equally, the light of the gospel that we believe as Jesus' followers not only illuminates our lives but also draws others to it, too. It reveals the true nature of whatever we bring into the light, whether good or bad, strong or weak, useful or a hindrance.

In today's world, where we try to avoid accusations of 'unfairness' at all costs, the final verse sounds troubling. The context is not, however, a crudely literal 'God helps those who help themselves'. We should think instead of Jesus' parable of the talents (Matthew 25:14–30), with its model of working with the 'master' who bestows gifts in order to multiply them, whether great or small. We have the gift of salvation in order to spread the good news of God's kingdom; it is not for our personal gratification alone. We should be careful how we listen, then, that we do not allow the truth merely to wash over us but allow it to take root within our hearts.

Reflection

Is there a danger that praying for 'revival fire to sweep the land' can actually be a way of dodging the hard work of personally lifting up the gospel light in our homes and communities?

NS

JOHN 21:9–13 (NRSV)

Lakeside barbecue

When [the disciples] had gone ashore, they saw a charcoal fire there, with fish on it, and bread. Jesus said to them, 'Bring some of the fish that you have just caught.' So Simon Peter went aboard and hauled the net ashore, full of large fish, a hundred and fifty-three of them; and though there were so many, the net was not torn. Jesus said to them, 'Come and have breakfast.' Now none of the disciples dared to ask him, 'Who are you?' because they knew it was the Lord. Jesus came and took the bread and gave it to them, and did the same with the fish.

This passage is rich in the deeper meanings and echoes of earlier episodes characteristic of John's Gospel. Richard A. Burridge (*The People's Bible Commentary: John*, BRF, 1998) points out how the Greek word for the charcoal fire is only used in one other place, for the fire in the courtyard where Peter betrayed Jesus (18:18), while the word for the fish cooking on the fire means the same sort of dried fish as in the feeding of the 5000 (6:9–11). The precise number of the fish has also taxed the ingenuity of commentators over many centuries.

While it is rewarding to explore a passage in such depth, it is still good to read it as a narrative, albeit one startling in its juxtaposition of divine and mundane. Here is the risen Jesus, a matter of weeks after the world-shattering events of the first Easter, and he is hosting a barbecue on the beach. The ordinary is hallowed, filled with powerful symbolism, by the presence of the Son of God, yet he also affirms the goodness of the ordinary by his actions. This is not magic fish or miraculous bread, but the everyday snack food of that culture. Equally, Jesus does not hold a prayer meeting or preach to his friends but simply shares a meal with them, as he would have done so often in the past. As then, times of such loving fellowship offer more than enough opportunity for the Spirit to move among us.

Reflection

If you are preparing a meal today, pause and think of Jesus being present with you, blessing the work of your hands.

NS

Revelation 1:12–16 (NRSV)

The blaze of glory

> Then I turned to see whose voice it was that spoke to me, and on turning I saw seven golden lampstands, and in the midst of the lampstands I saw one like the Son of Man, clothed with a long robe and with a golden sash across his chest. His head and his hair were white as white wool, white as snow; his eyes were like a flame of fire, his feet were like burnished bronze, refined as in a furnace, and his voice was like the sound of many waters. In his right hand he held seven stars, and from his mouth came a sharp, two-edged sword, and his face was like the sun shining with full force.

We finish these passages as we began them, with a symbolic vision of the Lord in glory—'one like a son of man' (as in Daniel 7:13–14, NIV). As Ezekiel fell on his face (1:28) and Isaiah cried 'Woe is me!' (6:5), so John admits (Revelation 1:17), 'I fell at his feet as though dead'. That is the only humanly possible response and, as we saw in our reading on Monday, in the presence of Almighty God, even the very heavens and the earth itself flee away.

'Seven' signifies completeness; white hair signifies the wisdom and authority that is the fruit of age; his eyes flash with what we would call the laser light of insight; the sword is double-edged, a lethal weapon. When we read that his face is 'like the sun shining with full force', we should think of the fiery heat of the noon sun in the southern Mediterranean or Turkey rather than the watery glow of a northern European summer.

Immediately after, however, we have the profound reassurance of the Holy One to the terrified mortal: 'Do not be afraid; I am the first and the last, and the living one. I was dead, and see, I am alive forever and ever' (vv. 17–18). That is the paradox of our faith right there: the Lord of heaven, blazing in full splendour, still comes close to soothe our fears and touch us with his eternal love.

Reflection and prayer

'Amen. Come, Lord Jesus!' (Revelation 22:20)

NS

1 John

One of my abiding memories, having been brought up in the country, is the sight of the winter night sky. Against the huge canopy of darkness, stars seemed to stand out with stunning clarity. Of course, you need the darkness, free from 'light pollution', actually to see the light.

In the first letter of John, the writer does something similar to describe some of the founding principles of the Christian faith, contrasting light and dark, love and hate, truth and falsehood and life and death. All of these things are brought together for one single (if multi-layered) purpose, which is that all who believe in the name of the Son of God may know that they have eternal life (1 John 5:13).

The letter seems to have been written because a church needed some reassurance. The author restates the message that had been received and transmitted by the apostles in order to give his audience renewed confidence in their faith. The problem appears to have been caused by the influence of some who have made claims for themselves that are different from the truths that the Church had come to believe. They may have claimed new revelations about God and Jesus or rejected some of the teaching of Christ or perhaps they simply had their own agendas and wanted to 'go it alone' without any interference from John or anyone else. John dismisses this group altogether and reminds the believers that the teaching they have received is indeed trustworthy.

Exactly who wrote this first letter cannot be known for sure. It may have been a disciple of John the apostle or another John who was part of his community. Certainly by the end of the second century, however, it came to be accepted as the work of the apostle John. Whatever the identity of the author, though, what is certain is that his message is enduring. The Church is still called to affirm and renew its life in the truth of God. Christians are to live out this truth and love God and one another. In this they have the help of his Spirit and an eternal hope.

Andrew John

Sunday 6 February

1 JOHN 1:1–4 (TNIV)

Living in a material world?

That which was from the beginning, which we have heard, which we have seen with our eyes, which we have looked at and our hands have touched—this we proclaim concerning the Word of life. The life appeared; we have seen it and testify to it, and we proclaim to you the eternal life, which was with the Father and has appeared to us. We proclaim to you what we have seen and heard, so that you also may have fellowship with us. And our fellowship is with the Father and with his Son, Jesus Christ. We write this to make our joy complete.

Christianity is probably the most materialistic of all religions. What I mean by this is not that the Christian faith is overly concerned with material things, but it is real and earthy. The opening verses of 1 John make this plain, describing something heard, seen and touched—very earthy things. This 'life' (v. 2), though, is also from the beginning and not only material but eternal.

Perhaps you are thinking that you have read something similar to these verses before. You would be right because they sound very much like the opening of John's Gospel. Here, though, the author brings just two great themes together: what is eternal and how the eternal became visible. Because God refused to remain in eternity and apart from hands that can touch and eyes that can see, we have fellowship with God (v. 3). Sharing in this joy is John's motivation.

At the start of the letter, we can see the heart of the Christian gospel: God has come to us in Jesus Christ and this has made a relationship with God possible. We call this idea 'grace' because it describes a free and voluntary act that is unmerited. John's introduction unpacks this idea beautifully, making it clear that you and I may have fellowship with God because the Word of Life came to us.

Prayer

Living Father, you have come to us through Jesus Christ, your Son. May we see and touch in such a way that our faith is strengthened and our understanding deepened through the one who is the Word of Life.

AJ

Being and doing

> God is light; in him there is no darkness at all. If we claim to have fellowship with him and yet walk in the darkness, we lie and do not live out the truth. But if we walk in the light, as he is in the light, we have fellowship with one another, and the blood of Jesus, his Son, purifies us from all sin. If we claim to be without sin, we deceive ourselves and the truth is not in us. If we confess our sins, he is faithful and just and will forgive us our sins and purify us from all unrighteousness. If we claim we have not sinned, we make him out to be a liar and his word is not in us.

We live in an age of slogans and soundbites, which are snappy and easier to communicate than long drawn-out ideas. In the realm of politics, however, they tend to be misleading and cover a multitude of sins!

Here we see that it is one thing to say and quite another to demonstrate something. John continues to tell us about grace and the God who is 'light' (v. 5), but he shows that we cannot claim an attachment to God who is light and yet live in darkness (v. 6). Conversely, if we deny that we sin, we not only deceive ourselves but also call God a liar.

Fellowship with God is not an occasional liaison—it means being like him and doing as he does. John can see a danger in this and it is despair. What if we get it wrong? Does that mean we cannot know God or, worse, ever have known him?

John's answer is that the same grace that came to us in Jesus provides cleansing from sin through his death. The idea of sacrifice is not an easy one for us today, but what it means here is that Jesus' death has been effective—wrongs are cancelled and an inner change takes place in Christians who acknowledge their weakness to God.

Prayer

Heavenly Father, help me see the connections between my faith and my life. Thank you that when I fall, I know you will help me through your Son Jesus Christ. Amen

AJ

1 JOHN 2:1–6 (TNIV)

More than words

My dear children, I write this to you so that you will not sin. But if anybody does sin, we have an advocate with the Father—Jesus Christ, the Righteous One. He is the atoning sacrifice for our sins, and not only for ours but also for the sins of the whole world. We know that we have come to know him if we keep his commands. Those who say, 'I know him,' but do not do what he commands are liars, and the truth is not in them. But if anyone obeys his word, love for God is truly made complete in them. This is how we know we are in him: whoever claims to live in him must live as Jesus did.

'Show me, don't tell me.' That is a phrase we probably can all relate to. It is not enough to be told something if we cannot make sense of it; we need to be shown to ensure understanding. John begins to deal with this issue here, but he also wants to underscore the message that he has been developing.

What does being 'sin-free' mean (v. 1)? John knows very well that this is an aim as well as a reality. Christians are called to a holy life (compare Matthew 5:48 or 1 Peter 1:15–16), but, when we sin, God does not leave us helpless. He provides a defence—namely Jesus, whose life, laid down in sacrifice, 'makes good' our sins.

How can we know that we truly belong to God and our failures are not evidence of being separated from him? John points out that those who belong to God practise what they preach; they are 'doers', not just 'hearers' (James 1:22). They find that God enables them to improve as his love grows in them (1 John 2:5).

There is both challenge and hope in these verses. Christian faith is a matter of doing Godlike things, but also discovering that help is at hand when we fail.

Prayer

Living God, teach me how to put faith into practice and to be more than a Christian of words. I'm grateful for your help and the way you forgive my sins. May this forgiveness lead me to a closer walk with you. Amen

AJ

Wednesday 9 February

1 JOHN 2:7–11 (TNIV)

Haven't we heard this before?

Dear friends, I am not writing you a new command but an old one, which you have had since the beginning. This old command is the message you have heard. Yet I am writing you a new command; its truth is seen in him and in you, because the darkness is passing and the true light is already shining. Those who claim to be in the light but hate a fellow believer are still in the darkness. Those who love their fellow believers live in the light, and there is nothing in them to make them stumble. But those who hate a fellow believer are in the darkness and walk around in the darkness; they do not know where they are going, because the darkness has blinded them.

I can remember my grandfather teaching me to fish. He needed a lot of patience! It involved looking after expensive equipment, learning about river conditions and coping with the endless tangles that accompanied my early attempts. Most of all, it involved watching him and learning. These verses show that there is no better way of learning than putting something into practice.

John is keen to show here that Christian faith is both in keeping with and also grows out of the Old Testament. It appears that these disciples had a Jewish background because John is able to state that the command he gives is not new, his readers would have known it 'from the beginning' (v. 7). Now it is visible in a new place or, more specifically, a person—Jesus—but also in the Christian believers.

This builds on what he has already said about being a person of action and not simply a disciple of words. What is new is the way John suggests that the light and truth are made visible in us. There are two aspects to this: Christians can see because they are not in darkness (v. 11) and (because they can see) they can make right choices. Being in darkness not only reveals our true condition but also makes it impossible for us to know and follow God.

Reflection

To what extent can Christ's light and truth be made visible in your life?

AJ

1 JOHN 2:12–17 (TNIV, ABRIDGED)

Faith essentials

I am writing to you, dear children, because your sins have been forgiven on account of his name. I am writing to you, fathers, because you know him who is from the beginning. I am writing to you, young people, because you have overcome the evil one. I write to you, dear children, because you know the Father. I write to you, fathers, because you know him who is from the beginning. I write to you, young people, because you are strong, and the word of God lives in you... Do not love the world... For everything in the world—the cravings of sinful people, the lust of their eyes and their boasting about what they have and do—comes not from the Father but from the world. The world and its desires pass away, but whoever does the will of God lives for ever.

Some of my earliest memories of faith are tied up with the hymns and songs we sang at church. I can remember chunks of the Bible and some solid teaching, all of which featured in sung worship.

Here, what appears to be a hymn encourages all kinds of Christians with truths about God and faith—sins forgiven through Christ, knowledge of God, victory over the 'evil one' and the abiding word of God in them. John deliberately repeats some of these truths to press the point home.

Most of us will at some point have prepared for an exam, performance or test, when needing to get the essentials straight is unavoidable. This is true in faith terms, too. We need these positive reminders of what God and we, by his grace, have achieved because there is a battle to be waged! John continues with a call to radical holiness (vv. 15–17), which is possible only if we are strong in the essentials of faith. Remember it is not the physical world that he has in mind, but all that is opposed to God. Our faith is nurtured in God's grace, which makes some hard choices possible. That is what it means to be a disciple.

Prayer

True and living God, may your strength overcome my weakness and my faith be always founded on what you have done for me. Amen

AJ

1 John 2:18–23 (TNIV, abridged)

Danger signs

This is how we know it is the last hour. They went out from us, but they did not really belong to us... But you have an anointing from the Holy One, and all of you know the truth. I do not write to you because you do not know the truth, but because you do know it and because no lie comes from the truth. Who is the liar? It is whoever denies that Jesus is the Messiah. Such a person is the antichrist—denying the Father and the Son. No one who denies the Son has the Father; whoever acknowledges the Son has the Father also.

Our eldest son had a passion for screwdrivers when he was very young. Unfortunately, he wanted to play with electrical sockets with said screwdrivers. It was extremely difficult to explain that the two did not go together (at least not in the way he wanted!). Although warnings are less palatable than pleasantries, they are probably more important.

Today's passage reminds us that John wrote this letter to counter the challenge of those who 'went out from us' (v. 19) and the danger of false teaching, which is anti Christ. He identifies this departure from the truth as a sign of 'the last hour' (v. 18). It is fair to ask what this means, given that Christ has not yet returned. It is equally fair to respond that John is using figurative language and does not give a detailed timetable because he is either unsure of it or does not think it relevant. Also, Jesus said that no one besides the Father knew the time of the Son's return (Matthew 24:36).

The false believers asserted that Jesus was not the Christ—a denial striking at the heart of faith and emptying Christianity of its essence. No wonder John refers to them as liars (1 John 2:22). We cannot reduce Jesus to the level of a good man, guide, philosopher or even prophet. That would utterly distort the Christian faith, the heart of which is Jesus Christ—the Son of the Father.

Prayer

Lord God, you have revealed the truth through your Son.
Give me steadfastness and resolve to hold only to what is true
and to rejoice in your unfailing goodness. Amen

AJ

1 JOHN 2:24–29 (TNIV, ABRIDGED)

Focus!

See that what you have heard from the beginning remains in you. If it does, you also will remain in the Son and in the Father. And this is what he promised us—eternal life... The anointing you received from him remains in you, and you do not need anyone to teach you. But as his anointing teaches you about all things and as that anointing is real, not counterfeit—just as it has taught you, remain in him. And now, dear children, continue in him, so that when he appears we may be confident and unashamed before him at his coming. If you know that he is righteous, you know that everyone who does what is right has been born of him.

I have always been impressed by people who show resolve and focus, be it in the world of sport, business, politics or faith. A good number do not always come across as easy or relaxing and would probably be quite difficult to work with, but they are not easily swayed by external pressures, which in itself can be admirable.

John exhorts his readers to remain focused and resolute because those who are in opposition to the Christian community were apparently trying to influence the believers to follow their direction (v. 26). John's response is robust: Christians are to stand firm. His key word here is 'remain', although the verb 'to continue' is also a good translation. He reminds his readers that the anointing they received (that is, their inclusion in Christ) remains. In other words, they have all they need to stand firm. This results in something much greater than winning an argument—eternal life is God's promise.

Today there are many pressures on us as Christians and we can feel overwhelmed and respond by accommodating whatever is creating the pressure. That is why John reminds his readers that what they have received is sufficient. What pressures threaten to move you from the sure ground of Christ? Whatever they are, God has more than enough to keep you firm.

Prayer

Heavenly Father, give me a wise and unshakeable faith in you. Teach me how to discern what is true and to find my strength to press on in your Son Jesus Christ. Amen

AJ

1 John 3:1–6 (TNIV, abridged)

When the clouds part

> See what great love the Father has lavished on us, that we should be called children of God!... Dear friends, now we are children of God, and what we will be has not yet been made known. But we know that when Christ appears, we shall be like him, for we shall see him as he is. All who have this hope in him purify themselves, just as he is pure. Everyone who sins breaks the law; in fact, sin is lawlessness. But you know that he appeared so that he might take away our sins. And in him is no sin. No one who lives in him keeps on sinning. No one who continues to sin has either seen him or known him.

Have you ever taken a walk on a rainy day and seen the sun shining through the clouds? There is that mix of warmth, the light all around you and the smell of rain on grass. Today's reading is a bit like that. After some important warnings, there is a note of unrestrained joy, like the parting of the clouds.

John reminds us that Christians are children of God and, therefore, inheritors of our Father's riches. In a world full of abandonment and alienation, we will never know anything more wonderful or important than this eternal belonging. Today, whatever else is happening in your life, hold on to the unalterable truth that you are a son or daughter of the God of all creation.

John also sees a connection between this and being a disciple. There is an end to sin (v. 6), in that, because we belong to him, we sin less. There is also a hope that purifies us as we wait for Christ's return (v. 3) as, although our lives in Christ are not obvious to the world, when Jesus appears, we will be like him (v. 2). Here, John is drawing on a tradition that to see God leaves God's imprint (compare 2 Corinthians 3:18). One day we shall truly be and be seen as the children of God.

Prayer

Lord Jesus Christ, you became human so that we might become like you.
Remind us daily of the privilege we share with all your people
and show us what this involves. Amen

AJ

1 JOHN 3:7–9, 13–15 (TNIV)

The hand of God

Dear children, do not let anyone lead you astray. The one who does what is right is righteous, just as he is righteous. The one who does what is sinful is of the devil, because the devil has been sinning from the beginning. The reason the Son of God appeared was to destroy the devil's work. Those who are born of God will not continue to sin, because God's seed remains in them; they cannot go on sinning, because they have been born of God… Do not be surprised, my brothers and sisters, if the world hates you. We know that we have passed from death to life, because we love each other. Anyone who does not love remains in death. Anyone who hates a fellow believer is a murderer, and you know that no murderers have eternal life in them.

In this passage, John brings out the consequences of faith in a dramatic way and shows, much as Jesus did, that what grows in a person reveals his or her true nature (compare Matthew 7:16–20).

The connection between actions and character provides a sort of identity test so that true and counterfeit Christians can be recognised. We know those born of God because we can see God's influence in their lives (1 John 3:9). This connection also gives us some confidence and hope, because it can be tempting to think that evil generally has the upper hand. The media bombard us with stories of terrible events, creating the impression that such trouble is the world's default setting, but John tells us the very opposite is true. How can this be the case?

Here we find ourselves in the spotlight: we reveal Christ! We must love our fellow Christians in such a way that reveals we have passed from death to life (v. 14). It is often said that we are the best adverts for God—and the worst. Will we advertise God's good or bad news?

Prayer

Father, give me today a sense of what is possible in and for you.
Give me new grace in decisions that I make so that evil is kept at bay
and goodness flourishes, for the sake of Jesus. Amen

AJ

1 JOHN 3:16–20, 23–24 (TNIV, ABRIDGED)

Good does work

This is how we know what love is: Jesus Christ laid down his life for us. And we ought to lay down our lives for one another... Dear children, let us not love with words or tongue but with actions and in truth. This is how we know that we belong to the truth and how we set our hearts at rest in his presence: if our hearts condemn us, we know that God is greater than our hearts, and he knows everything... And this is his command: to believe in the name of his Son, Jesus Christ, and to love one another as he commanded us. Those who keep his commands live in him, and he in them. And this is how we know that he lives in us: we know it by the Spirit he gave us.

One of my favourite artists is the Italian painter Caravaggio (1571–1610). He pioneered a way of contrasting light and dark to highlight themes that interested him. In one of his paintings, 'The seven works of mercy', he portrays a variety of people attending to the needs of others, drawing inspiration from one of Jesus' parables (Matthew 25:31–46). What is striking about the painting is how the people appear to be instinctively responding to human need. Similarly, in today's passage, John blends his theme of Christ's love for us with how we reflect that love to others.

He has already referred to Jesus' death as a saving event (1 John 2:1–2); he now stresses how it is an example. Being a Christian is not a matter of words alone, nor can we divide faith into good doctrine and good deeds because, if we truly know Jesus' love, we cannot but share it with others. John emphasises this relationship as a test of the truth that our love for one another demonstrates we belong to God.

He notes the comfort that this truth brings (3:19–20) and identifies its source as God's Spirit (v. 24). God is both the inspiration for our life through Jesus and the strength for responding through the Spirit.

Prayer

Heavenly Father, send your Spirit to sustain my response so that I am not anxious but confident, through him who is the perfect example, Jesus Christ. Amen

AJ

Wednesday 16 February

1 JOHN 4:1–6 (TNIV, ABRIDGED)

Proof of the pudding

Dear friends, do not believe every spirit, but test the spirits to see whether they are from God, because many false prophets have gone out into the world. This is how you can recognise the Spirit of God: every spirit that acknowledges that Jesus Christ has come in the flesh is from God, but every spirit that does not acknowledge Jesus is not from God… You, dear children, are from God and have overcome them, because the one who is in you is greater than the one who is in the world… We are from God, and whoever knows God listens to us; but whoever is not from God does not listen to us.

It must be a sign that I am getting older when I cannot understand things my children say! One of them had to explain the idea of 'eye candy' to me, that it is something or someone attractive to look at. What is true for the eye can be true for the lips, too—some words and phrases can appear intensely attractive (perhaps we should call this 'candy speak')—but is everything that sounds attractive always good?

John deals with this very point, making what is said and believed about Jesus the acid test of faith (v. 2). To deny Jesus is to deny God—it is a stand or fall issue on which we cannot hedge our bets. A truly human saviour is not an optional extra but a necessity, because the denial of Jesus' humanity strikes at the heart of salvation by putting distance between God and human beings. Christians believe that Jesus tasted death for everyone (Hebrews 2:9), but he could not do this if he only *appeared* to be human. We have hope, though, because God in us is stronger than those who would deny him (1 John 4:4).

It is not as easy to contend and be cautious as it is to affirm and approve, but here we see that discernment is a vital part of believing, exercised within the humble confidence that faith brings.

Prayer

Lord, give me a faith that sees what is true and what is false. Save me from thinking that I am always right; help me to judge everything against the truth of your Son, Jesus Christ. Amen

AJ

Thursday 17 February

1 John 4:12–15, 18–20 (TNIV)

Blogging or belonging?

No one has ever seen God; but if we love one another, God lives in us and his love is made complete in us. This is how we know that we live in him and he in us: he has given us of his Spirit. And we have seen and testify that the Father has sent his Son to be the Saviour of the world. If anyone acknowledges that Jesus is the Son of God, God lives in them and they in God… Perfect love drives out fear, because fear has to do with punishment. The one who fears is not made perfect in love. We love because he first loved us. If we say we love God yet hate a brother or sister, we are liars. For if we do not love a fellow believer, whom we have seen, we cannot love God, whom we have not seen.

Throughout this letter we have seen that faith in God is always faith in action. John has no aversion to repeating this message—just in case we do not pick up on it first time!

In today's passage, he makes two further important points, involving love for others. First, John describes this love as something 'seen' (v. 12), making the invisible, visible. This extraordinary idea means that Christians can reveal something of God in their lives.

I thank God for those who have shown me Christ through their Spirit-filled personalities and through a graciousness that is profoundly Christ-like. Anyone familiar with emails will relate to the idea of 'embedding' a picture or link in a message. Well, John shows us that love must be embedded in us if Christ is to be made visible.

Second, he shows how this love can grow and develop. It is not a static lump so much as a living creature that needs to be nurtured. Love can thus be deepened, but it can also weaken and die (Revelation 3:15–16) if neglected. Such love is not easy to manifest, but it is an incredible privilege to know that we can display Christ despite our weaknesses.

Prayer

Lord Jesus, be deeply embedded in my life in a way that helps others to see you. Give me what I need so that my love grows into you, whom I desire above earthly things. Amen

AJ

1 John 5:6–12 (TNIV, abridged)

Solid ground for faith

This is the one who came by water and blood—Jesus Christ... And it is the Spirit who testifies, because the Spirit is the truth. For there are three that testify: the Spirit, the water and the blood; and the three are in agreement. We accept human testimony, but God's testimony is greater because it is the testimony of God, which he has given about his Son. Whoever believes in the Son of God accepts this testimony. Whoever does not believe God has made him out to be a liar, because they have not believed the testimony God has given about his Son. And this is the testimony: God has given us eternal life, and this life is in his Son. Whoever has the Son has life; whoever does not have the Son of God does not have life.

Sometimes we know what someone is thinking before they speak, especially if we know them well. There is an instinctive response within us, despite the absence of words. Here, John identifies three elements in discerning the truth about salvation: water, the blood and the Spirit. It is not absolutely certain what he means by 'water', but it is likely that he is referring to Jesus' baptism and when he mentions 'blood', he means Jesus' death.

Although Jesus did not become the Son of God at his baptism (a view of some in the Early Church), his nature as the eternal Son of God is not an appendage to faith but its essence. He came by blood, too—that is, he died; his achievements are significant. Finally, it is the Spirit who testifies—that is, reveals the truth of these things. This picks up on our first point about instinct. Through the testimony of God's Spirit, our own understanding grows; we grasp this revelation because it is in harmony with what we already know about Jesus' nature and victory.

Once more, John is not concerned with doctrine in the abstract, but with providing a firm basis for faith. That is our inheritance as we seek to follow Jesus.

Prayer

Heavenly Father, thank you that your Son came to die for us.
Send your Spirit so that we might know the truth deep within our hearts and move forward, confident in our faith. Amen

AJ

1 John 5:16–21 (TNIV, abridged)

Life not death

> If you see any brother or sister commit a sin that does not lead to death, you should pray and God will give them life… There is a sin that leads to death. I am not saying that you should pray about that. All wrongdoing is sin, and there is sin that does not lead to death. We know that anyone born of God does not continue to sin; the One who was born of God keeps them safe… We know also that the Son of God has come and has given us understanding, so that we may know him who is true. And we are in him who is true by being in his Son Jesus Christ. He is the true God and eternal life. Dear children, keep yourselves from idols.

I remember writing letters to an older brother who was away at university, but, as I did not know how to start or finish, the letters began and ended abruptly. It is not that John had no idea how to write letters, but he ends as abruptly I used to!

The opening verses today look rather worrying, but, in the Gospels, we see the idea that it is only a deliberate refusal to believe that can prevent us from coming to God (Matthew 12:31). This appears to be what John means by the 'sin that leads to death'. His point is pastorally focused, however, because he exhorts concern for those going astray. In such situations, our first port of call is God and prayer because only God is able to turn their hearts towards himself.

We now come to that last blunt sentence, so different from the beauty of the opening of chapter 1! The two are connected, however, because idolatry means rejecting the Word of life in favour of created things. John ends in this way because he knows the temptations we face and the powers at work to defeat the Church. The great certainties he has described and our very being 'in him who is true' (5:20) call for the response of love and faith that he has been describing throughout his letter.

Prayer

Heavenly Father, as I live in your Son and he in me, write these truths deep within my being, for Jesus' sake. Amen

AJ

The miracles of Jesus in Matthew

Matthew, in his Gospel, is on a mission to reveal the authority of Jesus. First, he demonstrates that Jesus is the Son of God in his Sermon on the Mount, which left the crowds amazed. Then he moves from Jesus' words to his actions, detailing, in quick-fire succession, miracle after miracle after miracle. Through these, Jesus takes authority over nature, sickness, sin and demons, while pouring out his love and compassion on his people, whom he calls 'sheep without a shepherd' (Matthew 9:36). If the people were amazed at his teaching, imagine their reaction after witnessing a person's sight being restored or a leper cured.

Matthew's account is concise—he leaves out details in the stories that other Gospel writers fill in. By means of this brevity, Matthew hammers home his message about the Son of God on earth who is ushering in God's kingdom.

Jesus' miracles tend to fall into three categories: those controlling nature, those eradicating sickness (and even death) and those casting out demons. Contrary to the expectations of the disciples, the teachers of the law or his Jewish readers, Jesus extends his healing grace to the disaffected and outcast—even to the Gentiles. As Michael J. Wilkins says in his *NIV Application Commentary: Matthew* (Zondervan, 2004, p. 339), 'Jesus breaks down purity, ethnic, and gender barriers so that all may respond to his invitation to the kingdom of heaven'. Jesus stuns them with his words and works and makes them wonder, 'Who is this man?'

As I read through Matthew's account of Jesus' miracles, I was struck more than once by Jesus' compassion. When he sees the suffering of the people, he immediately brings peace of body and soul. He then reinforces this with his call to peace, one he still issues: 'Come to me, all you who are weary and burdened, and I will give you rest' (11:28).

Yes, Jesus works miracles today. Physical healings are spectacular, but emotional healings can also be life-altering, bringing freedom, joy and fulfilment. Do we have the faith to believe that Jesus can and will work in our own hearts and lives? I pray we will encounter the stories of Jesus' miracles that follow with an attitude of expectancy, reverence and gratitude.

Amy Boucher Pye

MATTHEW 8:1–4 (TNIV)

Be clean

> When Jesus came down from the mountainside, large crowds followed him. A man with leprosy came and knelt before him and said, 'Lord, if you are willing, you can make me clean.' Jesus reached out his hand and touched the man. 'I am willing,' he said. 'Be clean!' Immediately he was cleansed of his leprosy. Then Jesus said to him, 'See that you don't tell anyone. But go, show yourself to the priest and offer the gift Moses commanded, as a testimony to them.'

The crowds have just been amazed by Jesus' Sermon on the Mount and, here, we see him coming down the mountain, where they will be bowled over by his works, too. The first miracle that Matthew recounts brings restoration to one who has suffered from leprosy (or it might actually have been another skin disease). In Jewish law, those so afflicted would be called 'unclean' and banished to leper colonies, away from non-sufferers, to prevent the disease from spreading to others. The leprosy would continue to take over the sufferers' bodies until, finally, they would die.

Although the other miracles are called healings, this one is called a cleansing, for only Jesus could make a leprosy sufferer clean. Perhaps Matthew chose to recount this miracle first to show the Jewish people that Jesus is the fulfilment of the law (Mark and Luke first tell of Jesus driving a demon out of a man in Capernaum). After healing the man, Jesus tells him to show himself to the priest and offer the prescribed gift. By doing this he is signalling that one greater than Moses has come; he is ushering in a new order.

We could push this healing aside as not affecting us, but the spread of leprosy in a body is similar to the spread of sin in our lives. If we do not present ourselves to Jesus for cleansing, our sin will spread, separating us from each other and from God (as Michael Green says in *The Message of Matthew*, IVP, 1988, p. 114). Only Jesus can bring the cleansing that releases us into wholeness and makes us clean.

Prayer

Lord Jesus Christ, show me where sin may be lodging,
that I may be cleansed by your healing hand.

ABP

Monday 21 February

MATTHEW 8:5–10, 13 (TNIV)

First for the Jew, then for the Gentile

When Jesus had entered Capernaum, a centurion came to him, asking for help. 'Lord,' he said, 'my servant lies at home paralysed, suffering terribly.' Jesus said to him, 'Shall I come and heal him?' The centurion replied, 'Lord, I do not deserve to have you come under my roof. But just say the word, and my servant will be healed. For I myself am a man under authority, with soldiers under me. I tell this one, "Go," and he goes; and that one, "Come," and he comes. I say to my servant, "Do this," and he does it.' When Jesus heard this, he was amazed and said to those following him, 'Truly I tell you, I have not found anyone in Israel with such great faith...' Then Jesus said to the centurion, 'Go! Let it be done just as you believed it would.' And his servant was healed at that very hour.

Jesus continues to blow apart the people's preconceptions as he exercises his authority, bringing healing to the Gentiles. When a Roman soldier asks for help, Jesus responds by asking if he should go to his house to heal the man. The soldier, however, wants to avoid Jesus becoming ceremonially unclean from entering a Gentile home. So the centurion applies the principles of faith and authority to the situation. As a man under authority who obeys the words of his superiors and as one who has men serving under him, he believes that if Jesus just says the word, his servant will be healed.

So it was. This miracle signals that the new kingdom is not limited to Jewish people but available to Gentiles as well. It is also a stark warning to those in Israel who may have grown complacent in their status as the chosen people. Never, said Jesus, has he found someone of such great faith 'in Israel'. Those listening must have felt stunned by this remark.

Do we take our faith for granted? How could you exercise great faith this day?

Reflection

'I am not ashamed of the gospel, because it is the power of God that brings salvation to everyone who believes: first to the Jew, then to the Gentile' (Romans 1:16).

ABP

MATTHEW 8:23–27 (TNIV)

Lord of the wind and the waves

Then [Jesus] got into the boat and his disciples followed him. Suddenly a furious storm came up on the lake, so that the waves swept over the boat. But Jesus was sleeping. The disciples went and woke him, saying, 'Lord, save us! We're going to drown!' He replied, 'You of little faith, why are you so afraid?' Then he got up and rebuked the winds and the waves, and it was completely calm. The men were amazed and asked, 'What kind of man is this? Even the winds and the waves obey him!'

In his account, Matthew shows that Jesus is not only Lord over disease and demons but over nature, too. He is Immanuel, God with us, who rebukes the storm over the seas just as God in the Old Testament made the waters calm—see, for instance, Psalm 104:7 ('at your rebuke the waters fled') or Isaiah 50:2 ('by a mere rebuke I dry up the sea'). At his mere word the seas obey, causing the frightened disciples to wonder just who it is that is in the boat with them. They had seen him healing previously incurable diseases, but they had not reckoned on him controlling nature as well. Being familiar with the references in the Old Testament mentioned above, they would have realised immediately the gravity of Jesus' actions here.

The storm was also no ordinary storm. This is hinted at by the Greek word *seismos*, which usually means an earthquake or, literally, a 'shaking' (R.T. France, *Matthew*, IVP, 1985, p. 161). A force descended from outside, bringing chaos—that is, a squall came upon the lake, violently and suddenly. Jesus demonstrates his authority by calming it with a rebuke.

Jesus wants us to believe in his power to still the storms in our lives, whether created from outside or within. As we turn to him, whether in fear or in faith, and as we ask him to save us, he brings calm and peace, creating order from disorder.

Prayer

Lord, I confess that when I see the waves leaping at my boat,
I react with fear. Come and save me and increase my faith
in your goodness and grace.

ABP

MATTHEW 8:28–32 (TNIV)

Even the demons believe

When [Jesus] arrived at the other side in the region of the Gadarenes, two demon-possessed men coming from the tombs met him. They were so violent that no one could pass that way. 'What do you want with us, Son of God?' they shouted. 'Have you come here to torture us before the appointed time?' Some distance from them a large herd of pigs was feeding. The demons begged Jesus, 'If you drive us out, send us into the herd of pigs.' He said to them, 'Go!' So they came out and went into the pigs, and the whole herd rushed down the steep bank into the lake and died in the water.

Sickness, blindness, stormy lakes and now demons. Jesus and his friends arrive in a Gentile area, which is why a herd of pigs is grazing there. Again, Matthew cuts out excess details as he points squarely to Jesus' action of release instead of giving a lot of background information about the possessed men.

The demons knew immediately who they were encountering—the Son of God. They recognise his authority and plead to be released into the pigs (2000 of them, according to Mark's Gospel). He tells them to go and they do so dramatically, sacrificing the pigs in the process. The Jewish people with Jesus would not have been bothered by this loss, for they so disliked pigs that they would have put them in the same category as the demons. The Gentiles, however, were troubled and asked Jesus to leave. As one commentator says pointedly, 'all down the ages the world has been refusing Jesus because it prefers the pigs' (quoted in Wilkins, *The NIV Application Commentary: Matthew*, p. 354).

We can feel bad for the drowned pigs, but if we focus too much on them we will miss the point of the story—the authority of the Messiah over demons and freedom and restoration for troubled men. Also, we can ponder that Jesus allowed the demons to transfer to the pigs because it was not the appointed time. We do not know why he did not eradicate the evil then, but we know that one day he will.

Prayer

Lord Jesus Christ, Son of the living God, have mercy on me, a sinner.

ABP

MATTHEW 9:1–7 (TNIV)

Forgiveness of sins

> Jesus stepped into a boat, crossed over and came to his own town. Some men brought to him a paralysed man, lying on a mat. When Jesus saw their faith, he said to the man, 'Take heart, son; your sins are forgiven.' At this, some of the teachers of the law said to themselves, 'This fellow is blaspheming!' Knowing their thoughts, Jesus said, 'Why do you entertain evil thoughts in your hearts? Which is easier: to say, "Your sins are forgiven," or to say, "Get up and walk"? But I want you to know that the Son of Man has authority on earth to forgive sins.' So he said to the paralysed man, 'Get up, take your mat and go home.' Then the man got up and went home.

News of Jesus' healing was spreading, so concerned friends of a paralysed man decide to take him to Jesus for healing. Matthew does not tell us about the extraordinary measures the friends took to get the man to Jesus—lowering him through a hole in the roof (Mark 2:4)—for he wants to focus on the conversation between Jesus and the teachers of the law.

Jesus tells the man that his sins are forgiven, which immediately sets off alarm bells in the scribes and experts in Judaism. Forgiving sins can only be done by God, they know, which is why they accuse Jesus of blasphemy. Jesus, knowing their unspoken evil thoughts, responds. He knows that they believe people will not be healed unless their sins are forgiven. A way to show them his power as the Son of Man is to heal the paralysed man—and to forgive his sins.

Receiving forgiveness can bring about healing, sometimes even physical, but of course that does not mean people who are struggling with disease or deformity are riddled with unconfessed sin. We will only fully be free when we enter the land of no more tears or crying or death. Until then, however, we need to continue to present ourselves to Jesus, confessing our sins and receiving his cleansing forgiveness.

Prayer

Lord Jesus, what friends that man had to care for him so deeply!
Show me this day how I can show love to my friends.

ABP

Friday 25 February

Matthew 9:18–25 (TNIV)

Hope for the desperate

A synagogue leader came and knelt before [Jesus] and said, 'My daughter has just died. But come and put your hand on her, and she will live.' Jesus got up and went with him, and so did his disciples. Just then a woman who had been subject to bleeding for twelve years came up behind him and touched the edge of his cloak. She said to herself, 'If I only touch his cloak, I will be healed.' Jesus turned and saw her. 'Take heart, daughter,' he said, 'your faith has healed you.' And the woman was healed from that moment. When Jesus entered the synagogue leader's house and saw the noisy crowd and people playing pipes, he said, 'Go away. The girl is not dead but asleep.' But they laughed at him. After the crowd had been put outside, he went in and took the girl by the hand, and she got up.

In utter despair, a leader in the synagogue approaches Jesus for help because his daughter has died. Jesus agrees to go to his house and, as they make their way through the crowd to do so, a woman touches the hem of Jesus' cloak, believing that her non-stop bleeding will be healed as a result. Jesus responds to both with compassion: the woman is indeed healed; the girl is roused to life.

Both situations are desperate. Jairus, the synagogue leader, tried everything but his daughter still died. Still, he holds out hope that this miracle man can save her, as does the woman who has been bleeding for years. For twelve years, she has been an outcast from her community, for the bleeding makes her unclean. She has tried every type of medical cure available, to no avail.

Jesus has compassion on those at the margins of society. He does not penalise them for coming to him as a last resort; he responds quickly and powerfully. His actions signal a new kingdom, one in which grace on grace is poured on God's children—all of God's children, whether women, little girls, the blind or leprous or the elite of society. May we enter into this grace today.

Prayer

Lord Jesus, help me to see those who might feel ostracised or lonely and let me be your agent of love and grace.

ABP

Matthew 9:35–38 (TNIV)

A plentiful harvest

Jesus went through all the towns and villages, teaching in their synagogues, proclaiming the good news of the kingdom and healing every disease and illness. When he saw the crowds, he had compassion on them, because they were harassed and helpless, like sheep without a shepherd. Then he said to his disciples, 'The harvest is plentiful but the workers are few. Ask the Lord of the harvest, therefore, to send out workers into his harvest field.'

Today, we will not focus on one particular miracle, but, rather, look at one of the broad statements about Jesus' ministry. He has come to teach, proclaim and heal and his ministry is fuelled by his great compassion for the crowds of people who clamour to hear him speak and receive his healing touch. The Greek word for 'compassion' used in the original indicates a deep feeling in the gut, which conveys how strongly Jesus feels for his people.

Jesus longs to be their shepherd—a common image in the Old Testament for God's relationship with his people. Jesus offers to provide protection and sustenance, meeting their voiced and unvoiced needs. He then changes the metaphor to another familiar one from Hebrew scripture, telling his disciples that the harvest is ripe but more workers are needed.

What is our role? To pray—'ask the Lord of the harvest'. So often, we put prayer low on our list of priorities, sometimes by default due to the busyness of life. For some amazing and mysterious reason, though, God wants to hear us cry out to him and he will act on those prayers. As Alfred, Lord Tennyson wrote in 'Morte d'Arthur', 'More things are wrought by prayer than this world dreams of'.

What would intentional prayer look like for you today? Is someone coming to mind, even as you read this, for whom you should pray and perhaps fast? Maybe you could use a timer to signal the hours, then pause for a moment at the end of each hour and pray for that person. God delights in the cries of his people for him, however we choose to voice them.

Reflection

'Preach the gospel always; if necessary, use words' (Francis of Assisi).

ABP

MATTHEW 12:9–14 (TNIV)

Mercy, not sacrifice

Going on from that place, [Jesus] went into their synagogue, and a man with a shrivelled hand was there. Looking for a reason to accuse Jesus, they asked him, 'Is it lawful to heal on the Sabbath?' He said to them, 'If any of you has a sheep and it falls into a pit on the Sabbath, will you not take hold of it and lift it out? How much more valuable is a human being than a sheep! Therefore it is lawful to do good on the Sabbath.' Then he said to the man, 'Stretch out your hand.' So he stretched it out and it was completely restored, just as sound as the other. But the Pharisees went out and plotted how they might kill Jesus.

As we move through Matthew's Gospel, the clash between the Pharisees and Jesus intensifies. His claims and acts of authority incense them. Seeking to trap him, they ask him about whether or not it is right to heal on the sabbath and present to him a man with a withered hand. Jesus detects their secret thoughts. When he asks about a sheep falling into a pit, he is referring to a long debate that the Pharisees were having about what was lawful on the sabbath.

Jesus shows how he is more concerned with mercy than correct ritual and with human beings over animals. With a command he tells the man to stretch out his hand. The man had been a pawn of the Pharisees, but Jesus makes all things new.

Of course, the Pharisees are not overjoyed. Instead of rejoicing that the man can now use his hand, they plot to kill Jesus. They may have been remembering how God restored Moses' arm with one command (Exodus 4:6–7), realising that Jesus, with this action, is claiming his Messiahship.

With whom do we most identify in today's passage? Jesus, blowing away preconceptions and healing (and, no, I am not encouraging a Messiah-complex)? The man, argued over and yet restored? The experts in the Law, who could not overcome their prejudice and see the new work of God?

Reflection

'"I desire mercy, not sacrifice." For I have not come to call the righteous, but sinners' (Matthew 9:13).

ABP

MATTHEW 14:25–31 (TNIV)

Water walking

Shortly before dawn Jesus went out to them, walking on the lake. When the disciples saw him walking on the lake, they were terrified. 'It's a ghost,' they said, and cried out in fear. But Jesus immediately said to them: 'Take courage! It is I. Don't be afraid.' 'Lord, if it's you,' Peter replied, 'tell me to come to you on the water.' 'Come,' he said. Then Peter got down out of the boat, walked on the water and came towards Jesus. But when he saw the wind, he was afraid and, beginning to sink, cried out, 'Lord, save me!' Immediately Jesus reached out his hand and caught him.

Jesus had just fed a hungry crowd of 5000 people after a day of teaching and was exhausted. He sent the disciples to find shelter on the other side of the lake while he went to pray, but they encounter another squall and spend much of the night trying to cross the lake. Whereas before Jesus was in the boat when the storm arose, this time they are on their own. By now, however, they know that Jesus is interceding for them and will come to them.

When he does, it is in a miraculous way, walking on the water. The disciples, depleted from the previous day's ministry and exhausted from a night of being buffeted by the waves, wonder if they are seeing an apparition. Jesus reassures them and his 'It is I' could hearken back to Yahweh's statement of 'I am' from Hebrew scripture.

Then, Peter asks to walk to Jesus. Jesus commands him to come and he does! Only when he takes his eyes off Jesus does he realise that this is not humanly possible and starts to sink. He knows, though, to cry out to Jesus for help.

The feeding of the multitude and the amazing aquatic balancing act bring forth a unified response from the disciples: 'Truly you are the Son of God' (v. 33). Likewise, may we give him the authority in our lives, turning to him when we are exhausted or sinking—or, even, when we are flying high.

Prayer

'I do believe; help me overcome my unbelief!' (Mark 9:24)

ABP

Tuesday 1 March

MATTHEW 15:22–28 (TNIV, ABRIDGED)

Crumbs to the dogs

A Canaanite woman from that vicinity came to [Jesus], crying out, 'Lord, Son of David, have mercy on me! My daughter is demon-possessed and suffering terribly.' Jesus... answered, 'I was sent only to the lost sheep of Israel.' The woman came and knelt before him. 'Lord, help me!' she said. He replied, 'It is not right to take the children's bread and toss it to the dogs.' 'Yes it is, Lord,' she said. 'Even the dogs eat the crumbs that fall from their master's table.' Then Jesus said to her, 'Woman, you have great faith! Your request is granted.'

I struggle to understand why Jesus took so long to heal the poor woman's daughter and why he may have employed the Jewish derogatory term of 'dogs' to describe the Gentiles. As Michael Green comments in *The Message of Matthew*, however, we do not know Jesus' inflection or delivery of his words for, in the Greek, punctuation is inferred and not written. So, Jesus could have been musing, asking if he was sent only to Israel. As Green says, 'I believe this was a soliloquy of Jesus' (p. 172).

However we interpret it, we know that Jesus' first mission was to save Israel. His actions here tell us, however, that he does not limit his grace. As with the Roman centurion who sought healing for his servant, Jesus admires this woman's faith and tenacity and heals her daughter.

The early Church would have been encouraged by this encounter, for it shows how amazed Jesus was by a Gentile's faith. The story would have also served as a warning to those in Israel who were complacent in their privileged status. What Jesus yearns for, as we see here, is great faith.

Passages like this one remind us that, as much as we would sometimes like to put Jesus into a neat and tidy box, we simply cannot do so. What we can do is follow the example of the Gentile woman, who was motivated by her maternal love and persevered in seeking healing for her daughter. We can also trust that God's love and mercy are sufficient—whatever our ethnicity, nationality or social tribe.

Prayer

Lord, thank you for the tenacity of this mother
and your loving response to her.

ABP

Wednesday 2 March

MATTHEW 17:14–18 (TNIV)

'I believe; help my unbelief'

When they came to the crowd, a man approached Jesus and knelt before him. 'Lord, have mercy on my son,' he said. 'He has seizures and is suffering greatly. He often falls into the fire or into the water. I brought him to your disciples, but they could not heal him.' 'You unbelieving and perverse generation,' Jesus replied, 'how long shall I stay with you? How long shall I put up with you? Bring the boy here to me.' Jesus rebuked the demon, and it came out of the boy, and he was healed from that moment.

A desperate father seeks help from Jesus' disciples and meets only with frustration. We do not know what the disciples had done for the boy, but Jesus saw immediately their lack of faith. It is this faithlessness that Matthew wants to highlight in his Gospel, for he again gives a sparse account in comparison with the other synoptic Gospels.

I can feel this father's pain, for it is a burden my own father and mother have had to bear. My brother has suffered from epilepsy since he was three years old and, although my parents have sought healing from the Lord, my brother still receives medical treatment for this condition. Why God heals sometimes and not always is one of the biggest mysteries of our faith. I can only put it down to the ongoing effects of the Fall, when sin, disease and death entered the universe.

In terms of my brother and this story, I do not believe he is demon-possessed, but that his suffering is in some way associated with our fallen world. We ask God to heal and desire that he will do so. When he does not, we continue to ask him to increase our faith, but, also, give us the wisdom to know when to accept that healing may not come this side of heaven.

Have you pleaded with the Lord for something, but your cries seem to have fallen on deaf ears? May your trust in God continue to grow and may he give you wisdom and understanding.

Prayer

Father God, we do not always understand. Enlarge our grasp of your truth and your love, and give us your peace.

ABP

MATTHEW 17:24–27 (TNIV)

Submission

After Jesus and his disciples arrived in Capernaum, the collectors of the two-drachma temple tax came to Peter and asked, 'Doesn't your teacher pay the temple tax?' 'Yes, he does,' he replied. When Peter came into the house, Jesus was the first to speak. 'What do you think, Simon?' he asked. 'From whom do the kings of the earth collect duty and taxes—from their own children or from others?' 'From others,' Peter answered. 'Then the children are exempt,' Jesus said to him. 'But so that we may not cause offence, go to the lake and throw out your line. Take the first fish you catch; open its mouth and you will find a four-drachma coin. Take it and give it to them for my tax and yours.'

Jesus' miracle here is not a healing, nor an exorcism, but one that becomes a teaching tool for Peter. The temple tax men had come to collect their dues (these were different from the tax collectors for the Roman occupiers, such as Matthew had been). Jesus knows that he is technically exempt from the tax for, as the Son of God, he need not pay for the upkeep of God's house. Nevertheless, he subjects himself to the law to avoid causing offence among the Jewish people.

Jesus could have claimed his rights as God's Son at this point, but he freely relinquishes them. By doing so, he prefigures his ultimate sacrifice—his death on the cross. There he submits to the earthly authorities and to his heavenly Father by relinquishing not only his rights but also his whole being.

As God's children who live in the freedom brought to us by Jesus, we are no longer bound by the rules and regulations that the ancient Israelites were subject to. We remain under authority, however, whether heavenly or earthly. May we thus pay our taxes without complaining and may we support our churches with the funds that the Lord provides for us—sometimes miraculously.

Prayer

Lord, all we have comes from you. Help us to spend our money wisely, becoming rich in heaven, and grant wisdom to the rulers of our nations and our churches, that they may be wise stewards of what you have given.

ABP

Matthew 15:30–37 (TNIV, abridged)

How many loves have you?

> Great crowds came to [Jesus], bringing the lame, the blind, the crippled, the mute and many others, and laid them at his feet; and he healed them... Jesus called his disciples to him and said, 'I have compassion for these people; they have already been with me three days and have nothing to eat...' His disciples answered, 'Where could we get enough bread in this remote place to feed such a crowd?' 'How many loaves do you have?' Jesus asked. 'Seven,' they replied, 'and a few small fish.'... He took the seven loaves and the fish, and when he had given thanks, he broke them and gave them to the disciples, and they in turn to the people. They all ate and were satisfied.

Jesus has been healing and teaching the crowds in Gentile territory. He sees that they are tired and hungry and is moved by compassion for them. He wants to meet not only their spiritual needs but also their physical ones. Although the disciples have already witnessed Jesus feeding the 5000, they still wonder how Jesus will feed these 4000 men, plus women and children. Jesus takes what the people give—seven small loaves and a few fish—and makes it sufficient for all. He multiplies their meagre offering into a feast that satisfies.

Let us note two things regarding this well-known miracle. First, Jesus performs it in Gentile territory. Although he came first of all for the Jewish people, he also yearns for non-Jews to eat and be satisfied by his food.

Second, Matthew indicates that this miracle points to Jesus breaking the bread during his last supper—Jesus takes, breaks the bread, gives thanks and offers it to the disciples. They, in turn, offer it to the people. We, too, should offer what we have to Jesus for distribution among his people. It might seem far too small or insignificant to satisfy the hunger that we see around us, but, as we read here, Jesus has a way of multiplying our 'bread' beyond our wildest imagination.

Prayer

Lord, on this Women's World Day of Prayer, we lift before you
the needs of Chile. Where we have loaves and fish to offer,
let us give that you may multiply them.

ABP

MATTHEW 17:1–8 (TNIV, ABRIDGED)

'My Son, whom I love'

After six days Jesus took with him Peter, James and John the brother of James, and led them up a high mountain by themselves. There he was transfigured before them. His face shone like the sun, and his clothes became as white as the light. Just then there appeared before them Moses and Elijah, talking with Jesus... A bright cloud covered them, and a voice from the cloud said, 'This is my Son, whom I love; with him I am well pleased. Listen to him!' When the disciples heard this, they fell face down to the ground, terrified. But Jesus came and touched them. 'Get up,' he said. 'Don't be afraid.' When they looked up, they saw no one except Jesus.

During the past two weeks, we have encountered Jesus' miracles, whether they were healing the sick, raising the dead, overcoming nature or exorcising demons. Our final miracle is the transfiguration, when the divine nature of Jesus is revealed. Whereas the other miracles are ones that Jesus performs, this one is performed on Jesus.

Jesus has taken his inner circle of disciples—those who were to be future church leaders—up a mountain to pray. It's as if the heavens open and their eyes are opened as they glimpse Jesus as God the Son, with his face shining and his clothes as white as light. Then they hear God say that this is his beloved Son and they should listen to him. As with all mortals who come in contact with the living God, they are terrified, but Jesus touches them, reassuring them. They are changed, but they are not to be afraid.

'Listen', says God the Father. Are we listening to Jesus? Do we stop to pause and wait for his words and his directions, in things big and small? Have we aligned our lives in submission to his loving will?

As we do so, Jesus will work miracles in us. As God's beloved Son, he promises to bring reconciliation, healing and restoration. May we enjoy the new kingdom that he is ushering in to its fullness, sharing his joy and peace with our families and those whom we meet.

Reflection

'For in him we live and move and have our being' (Acts 17:28).

ABP

The Lord's Prayer

When I was an English literature student, I read the works of the mystics, such as *The Cloud of Unknowing* and *The Ladder of Perfection*. They gave me the idea that, to pray properly, you have to practise a high level of concentration and dedication, which can enable you to enter in to a state of contemplation. I spent years trying to accomplish this feat. To be fair, I do not think that is what they were really teaching!

When Jesus starts to teach his disciples to pray (Luke tells us that it was at their request), he starts with a simple poem, for that is what the Lord's Prayer really is. Like biblical prophecy, it shows all the characteristics of Hebrew poetry, especially the way in which each section has two halves expressing the same thought.

Is this something that they are meant to learn by heart and recite daily? It can certainly be profitably used that way. Simone Weil, a 20th-century Jewish mystic and philosopher who was deeply drawn to Christ, set herself the task of learning it by heart in its original Greek, as she felt that brought her closer to Jesus' spirit. Whatever language it is in, it is also a model for all our prayers: we are to express our love to God, our heavenly Father; plead for God to bring in a better world; ask for what we need; confess our sins and pray for strength to meet challenges.

In the pages that follow, I explore this comprehensive prayer by linking it to passages from elsewhere in scripture, often themselves pieces of poetry. Sometimes they parallel a particular clause of the prayer; sometimes they contrast with it. I begin by looking at its context in the Sermon on the Mount, where Jesus critiques the way that the religious leaders of the time prayed and offers an alternative. I have, however, left out the 'doxology' at the end ('For the kingdom, the power and the glory are yours'), which does not appear in the original manuscripts, although it was prayed from early on in the Church's history.

While we are used to using Jesus' prayer in a public situation, it is also a private conversation between ourselves and God. Yet, we must never forget that it begins with 'Our' and encompasses the needs of the whole world. It is a brilliant model for all our prayers.

Veronica Zundel

MATTHEW 6:5–8 (NRSV, ABRIDGED)

A secret date with God

[Jesus said] 'And whenever you pray, do not be like the hypocrites; for they love to stand and pray in the synagogues and at the street corners, so that they may be seen by others... But whenever you pray, go into your room and shut the door and pray to your Father who is in secret; and your Father who sees in secret will reward you. When you are praying, do not heap up empty phrases as the Gentiles do; for they think that they will be heard because of their many words. Do not be like them, for your Father knows what you need before you ask him.'

In Britain, prayers are meant to be said before each school day, as well as in the Houses of Parliament before debating. Some of us think that this unhelpfully perpetuates the myth that this is a 'Christian country'. Meanwhile, in the USA, where Church and state are meant to be separate, Christians campaign to get prayer into schools and Congress.

Using the Lord's Prayer in isolation, we may forget that, in Matthew's Gospel, it is actually part of the Sermon on the Mount, where Jesus overturns many perceptions of what it means to be a disciple. His hearers might have assumed that letting others see you pray is a mark of holiness and the longer the prayer, the more likely it is to be answered. Some of us may even still assume this!

Of course, I do not think we should ban praying out loud in church, but Jesus here seems to be saying that the heart of prayer is a private, intimate relationship. To ask someone how his or her prayer life is, then, might be a bit like asking, 'When did you last sleep with your spouse?' It's ironic that the prayer he gave us as a model of how our prayers should be has become mainly a public prayer.

Given that this is the case, is it odd to use a 'set prayer' in our private devotions? No more odd than quoting a famous love poem to convey your love to your sweetheart. Indeed, many of us find that the words of others express our sentiments best.

Reflection

What elements covered in the Lord's Prayer might be missing from our private prayer?

VZ

MATTHEW 6:9A; HOSEA 11:1–4 (NRSV, ABRIDGED)

A big family

> 'Pray then in this way: Our Father in heaven...'
> When Israel was a child, I loved him, and out of Egypt I called my son... It was I who taught Ephraim to walk, I took them up in my arms; but they did not know that I healed them. I led them with cords of human kindness, with bands of love. I was to them like those who lift infants to their cheeks. I bent down to them and fed them.

The next book I write will be about the things we can learn about God from being a parent. Jesus' prime image for God is 'the Father', so thinking about human parents is a good way to think about God—even if we had inadequate parenting (or feel inadequate as parents ourselves or cannot be parents), we have an idea of what a good parent would be and do.

In my church we have just heard a series of sermons on the Lord's Prayer. In the first one, the preacher pointed out that the first word in Jesus' 'model prayer' is not 'My' but 'Our'. Having a personal relationship with God does not mean that such a relationship is our private possession—we share it with Christians around the world and through history.

Does this contradict what we were thinking yesterday about prayer being a private matter? No, because when we 'go into our room and shut the door', we are not alone but in the company of millions who are praying at the same time, as well as all those who have prayed before us.

So, having a divine parent gives us millions of sisters and brothers around the world. No Christian is an only child. God, as the reading from Hosea tells us, is less like the stereotype of a Victorian father with a stick ready to beat us and more like the mother of a toddler who has her child on a leading rein to help it learn to walk. I missed my son's first steps, as my back was turned, but God recorded them.

Reflection

Before God we are all toddlers.

VZ

MATTHEW 6:9; 7:21–23 (NRSV)

In God's name!

'Hallowed be your name.' ... 'Not everyone who says to me, "Lord, Lord," will enter the kingdom of heaven, but only one who does the will of my Father in heaven. On that day many will say to me, "Lord, Lord, did we not prophesy in your name, and cast out demons in your name, and do many deeds of power in your name?" Then I will declare to them, "I never knew you; go away from me, you evildoers."'

There is a story of a church plaque that bore the Lord's Prayer, but, because of the place where the line was broken, the first line read 'Our Father in Heaven, Hallo'. I think we sometimes treat this clause of the prayer as little more than a polite greeting or a pious wish that God's name should not be abused.

It seems to me, however, that the Lord's Prayer is not so much about what we do with God's name (for instance, using it as a swear word) but what we do in God's name. Is God honoured when some of us preach rejection and hatred for particular groups of people and call it Christian? Was God honoured when a nuclear submarine was christened (and I use the word 'christened' advisedly here) Corpus Christi ('the body of Christ')? Is it really in God's name when some of us teach that being a Christian is a way to become rich and prosperous?

Certainly, we should not be using the name of Jesus as a curse, but we also need to be very careful that the things we do, the lives we live in the name of Christ are truly in the spirit of Christ.

Of course, if we are already asking the question, 'Are our actions Christlike?', then they probably are. Those who are sure they are right are sometimes the most wrong. It is like the 'sin against the Holy Spirit'—if you think you have committed it, you can be pretty sure that you have not. Actually, in context (Matthew 12:22–32), it is pretty clear that to sin against the Spirit is to call good things evil—and perhaps vice versa.

Prayer

Lord, fill my actions with your Spirit, so they are worthy to bear your name.

VZ

MATTHEW 6:10; ISAIAH 11:6–9 (NRSV, ABRIDGED)

The longed-for kingdom

'Your kingdom come. Your will be done, on earth as it is in heaven.'

The wolf shall live with the lamb, the leopard shall lie down with the kid, the calf and the lion and the fatling together, and a little child shall lead them... The nursing child shall play over the hole of the asp, and the weaned child shall put its hand on the adder's den. They will not hurt or destroy on all my holy mountain; for the earth will be full of the knowledge of the Lord as the waters cover the sea.

In the middle of a Communion service with around 20,000 people, in a field at the Greenbelt Christian festival, it occurred to me that the phrase, 'Your kingdom come' should really be prayed as a wild shout, a cry of anguish and longing for a better world. While 'Your will be done' sounds like a fatalistic acceptance of what must be, it is really a desperate plea for a world different from this one, which is in pain in so many ways and corrupted by so many evils.

That different world is described in Isaiah's vision, often called 'the peaceable kingdom' and beautifully portrayed in a classic painting of this name by the naïve artist Edward Hicks (1780–1849). In this work of art, a toddler leads a tiger, while another strokes a leopard's nose and, in the background, a group of Quakers meet to make a treaty with Native Americans (which indeed they did in real life).

Today, Ash Wednesday, many churches make a cross sign with ashes on the foreheads of worshippers, accompanied by the sobering sentence, 'Remember that you are dust, and to dust you shall return.' I've always found those words rather comforting—to realise that I am a mere mortal and very little depends on me—but they can also remind us to look forward to a renewed, perfected resurrection life.

'Your kingdom come', however, is not about some heavenly realm beyond, but God's will being done on earth. The kingdom is not a disembodied afterlife but a transformed earth, a world without hunger or violence, where all live to worship and serve God. Something worth crying out for.

Prayer

How long, O Lord, how long?

VZ

Thursday 10 March

MATTHEW 6:11; PSALM 104:21, 24–28 (NRSV, ABRIDGED)

Bread for the world

'Give us this day our daily bread.'

The young lions roar for their prey, seeking their food from God... O Lord, how manifold are your works! In wisdom you have made them all; the earth is full of your creatures. Yonder is the sea, great and wide, creeping things innumerable are there, living things both small and great... These all look to you to give them their food in due season; when you give to them, they gather it up; when you open your hand, they are filled with good things.

I don't think we really know how to pray this part of the Lord's Prayer in the affluent, well-fed West. Maybe homeless people can pray it, but most of us know exactly where our daily bread is coming from and it is not God, but the supermarket, baker's or corner shop. Round the world, though, millions of people are hungry every day and they can pray this with real sincerity.

The rest of us may have other, less immediately physical needs. The lonely single person who wonders where the next hug is coming from; the exhausted carer who wonders where she will find new strength for the day—they can pray for their 'daily bread' in the knowledge that only God can supply comfort and courage.

It is reassuring that the Lord's Prayer is not all about the world and other people. We are allowed to pray, in direct and honest terms, for ourselves. Whatever 'bread' we hunger for, literal food or food for our souls, we can trust God to provide, just as, the psalmist suggests, God provides for the animals.

Who will actually feed the starving? In the TV series *Lark Rise to Candleford*, a rather dotty old man had a vision that pies and sausages would fall from the sky for the poor of Lark Rise. It did not happen, of course; that is not the way God works. Parcels of food do fall from helicopters, however, because human beings have donated and other human beings have worked to meet the need. Perhaps 'give us our daily bread' is one of those prayers we partly have to answer ourselves.

Prayer

'Give food to all those who are hungry, and hunger for justice to those who are fed' (from a sung grace).

VZ

MATTHEW 6:12; ACTS 15:37–40 (NRSV)

Falling out

'And forgive us our debts, as we also have forgiven our debtors.'

Barnabas wanted to take with them John called Mark. But Paul decided not to take with them one who had deserted them in Pamphylia and had not accompanied them in the work. The disagreement became so sharp that they parted company; Barnabas took Mark with him and sailed away to Cyprus. But Paul chose Silas and set out, the believers commending him to the grace of the Lord.

Why on earth have I linked a prayer for forgiveness with a rather unsettling story about conflict between the apostles? There's no obvious connection, is there?

I thought of Paul and Barnabas' story when I came to this section of the Lord's Prayer, though, because it reminds me that, even among the exalted company of the apostles, there was conflict and a need for forgiveness. After all, they were only human (Acts 14:13–15, where they dissuade the people of Lystra from worshipping them as pagan gods).

Polite English people are very good at hiding hurt feelings and pretending everything is all right. God is not English, however, and neither were Paul and Barnabas. They probably did quite a bit of shouting and waved their hands about before they reached an amicable solution, to split into two teams. The presence of a plea for forgiveness in his prayer shows that Jesus was realistic about the fact that we would sin and fight and so we would need forgiveness from each other as well as from God.

Does our being forgiven by God depend on us forgiving others first? The Lord's Prayer certainly makes it look that way. I think that, unless we are in a place of forgiveness ourselves, we will find it difficult to experience God's forgiveness. Many of my fellow Mennonites are trained in mediation and, thus, expert in helping those in conflict listen to each other and move on. We need more of this in our war-torn world—and our divided Church.

Reflection

'Put away from you all bitterness and wrath and anger and wrangling and slander, together with all malice, and be kind to one another, tender-hearted, forgiving one another, as God in Christ has forgiven you' (Ephesians 4:31–32).

VZ

Matthew 6:13; 1 Peter 4:12–13 (NRSV)

The trials of life

'And do not bring us to the time of trial, but rescue us from the evil one.'

Beloved, do not be surprised at the fiery ordeal that is taking place among you to test you, as though something strange were happening to you. But rejoice in so far as you are sharing Christ's sufferings, so that you may also be glad and shout for joy when his glory is revealed.

An old Jewish story tells of a man who asked God to give him back his dead son. God said he would do it if the man could find one household that had not known any suffering. He could not, of course.

Those who saw Jesus crucified would have had a very good idea of what 'the time of trial' meant, along with their later followers who experienced the gladiators' arena and other forms of persecution. We, who live an unbelievably comfortable life compared to most of the world, may feel that we do not know much about suffering, but, the older we become, the more likely we are to experience some situation we thought we could no longer bear and yet we probably did, with God's help.

Jesus teaches us to pray that we will not have to live through such times. Though suffering can be an experience that teaches us more about God and, thus, in some way, a 'discipline' (Hebrews 12:7), the Lord's Prayer gives us permission to plead to be spared. He knows what it is like to be desperate—just think of the garden of Gethsemane.

What about 'the evil one'? Is there such a force in the world, from which we need to be delivered? Jesus certainly thought so. Through a difficult situation at my son's school, I have learned recently that enemy love can only be practised when you have some enemies! I need to remember that it is not the perpetrator who is evil, only the actions.

'Rescue us!' is another of those heartfelt cries that can only be truly prayed by those in distress. May we rarely need to pray it.

Reflection

'For we do not have a high priest who is unable to sympathise with our weaknesses, but we have one who in every respect has been tested as we are, yet without sin' (Hebrews 4:15).

VZ

Bible stories rediscovered: Joseph

To study Joseph, you have to be prepared to travel. You will have to go to a land, a culture and a time that you know very little about, which means the journey will have to be in your imagination.

You will have to put aside all ideas of the West End musical, school productions and notions of dreamcoats, wonderful though they may have been. You will meet a young man from ancient history who was as alive as any of us and knew what it was to be loved and hated, trusted and respected, who flirted with death and with whom women flirted, who was forgotten in prison, then exalted as the most prominent in the land.

The Joseph story takes up a big chunk of the book of Genesis, which, after the opening creation and flood stories, tells us about the great family story of Abraham. Genesis takes us into the many adventures of Abraham and his family, then focuses on his son Isaac, before spending time with Isaac's twin sons, Jacob and Esau. We follow Jacob's fortunes with his eventual marriage to his beloved Rachel. An ongoing heartache in this story is that Rachel finds herself unable to have children, so she encourages Jacob to have children via his other wife, Leah, and two maidservants. However, in time, Rachel does conceive and gives birth to Joseph, who is especially favoured.

In the next two weeks, we shall come to know this young man better. One distinctive feature we will notice right from the start is that Joseph had the ability to see beyond the surface of things. He was always on the lookout for the deeper message as he used the eyes of his heart to see. Above all, or perhaps beneath all, he used the eyes of his heart in the darkness of night, in his dreams.

As we read the stories about him, we need to do what Joseph did so well: listen to the deeper message. In doing so, we will find that we do not just meet an interesting figure in the Bible but also a person very much for our times, with a word for each of us.

Michael Mitton

Sunday 13 March

Genesis 37:3–4 (TNIV)

The beloved son

Now Israel loved Joseph more than any of his other sons, because he had been born to him in his old age; and he made a richly ornamented robe for him. When his brothers saw that their father loved him more than any of them, they hated him and could not speak a kind word to him.

Joseph's father, Jacob, had his name changed to 'Israel'. The name means 'one who struggles with God' and it was given to him after his famous all-night wrestling match with God (Genesis 32:22–32). This wrestler-with-God has a particularly close relationship with Joseph because this son feels like a very special gift, given to him in his old age, and he is the first-born of his much beloved wife, Rachel.

Joseph's eleven brothers and sister were left in no doubt that their father especially loved Joseph. Jacob was not shy about showing this favouritism, making a special robe for him. The robe was very different from the normal, everyday cloak-like wrap that everyone else wore. It was distinguished by being much longer than normal cloaks and lavishly decorated. As a result it was a luxury that only the wealthy could afford. When Joseph wore the robe, he most certainly stood out in a crowd, especially when the crowd happened to be his brothers.

It is not difficult for us to imagine the depth of jealousy that this would have engendered. Even the most well-functioning family would struggle in such circumstances. Jacob, however—who has struggled with God and, indeed, with his own twin brother, Esau—is not concerned about creating potential conflict. Perhaps in that extraordinary wrestling match with God, Jacob finally found out what it was to be utterly loved by God. In turn, he wanted to give the same kind of love. We may disapprove of the fact that he ended up favouring one over the others, but at least he managed to love one of his children deeply. His fault was not in loving Joseph so much but in not allowing his heart to grow in love so that he could reach out to his other children as well.

Prayer

Lord, give me the courage to love and make my heart generous.

MM

GENESIS 37:5–8 (TNIV)

Dream on, son

Joseph had a dream, and when he told it to his brothers, they hated him all the more. He said to them, 'Listen to this dream I had: we were binding sheaves of corn out in the field when suddenly my sheaf rose and stood upright, while your sheaves gathered round mine and bowed down to it.' His brothers said to him, 'Do you intend to reign over us? Will you actually rule us?' And they hated him all the more because of his dream and what he had said.

One family trait Joseph seems to have inherited from his father is a complete lack of tact. As he strolled around wearing his glorious robe, it cannot have escaped his notice that his brothers were feeling somewhat put out. Most of us would have tried to mitigate the problem, but not Joseph. Instead, he tells them about his dream that one day he will be a big sheaf and they will be little sheaves bowing down to him. Rubbing salt into the wound, he then tells them about a second dream (v. 9), when the sun, moon and eleven stars bow down to him. Even his doting father is upset by this as he interprets this as meaning that he is the sun in the dream (v. 10).

Why does Joseph tell them about these dreams? Is it to tell them to watch out because one day they will be put in their places? Is he delivering a threat? Notice that he makes no real claims about the dreams. He does not claim that they are from God or prophetic, even though they turn out to be so. Maybe he genuinely does not know what to do with them, so he asks his family. He is, after all, only 17. He has a lot to learn.

What Joseph is convinced about is that the dreams are saying something significant, not just to him but also to others. He has learned to value the deeper levels of meaning revealed in the language of dreams. What he has to learn is how to share what he is hearing, especially to people who hear only what they want to hear.

Reflection

How can you listen to the deeper meaning?

MM

GENESIS 37:14, 17–20 (TNIV, ABRIDGED)

Monstrous jealousy

[Jacob] said to [Joseph], 'Go and see if all is well with your brothers and with the flocks, and bring word back to me'... Joseph went after his brothers and found them near Dothan. But they saw him in the distance, and before he reached them, they plotted to kill him. 'Here comes that dreamer!' they said to each other. 'Come now, let's kill him and throw him into one of these cisterns and say that a ferocious animal devoured him. Then we'll see what comes of his dreams.'

'O, beware, my lord, of jealousy', says Shakespeare's Iago to Othello, then goes on to call it 'the green-eyed monster which doth mock the meat it feeds on'. Our story of Joseph here develops the feel of a Shakespearean tragedy as the festering jealousy, which has been building up over years, reaches monstrous proportions and the brothers plot to kill the favoured son. Rather than murder, they decide to sell their brother as a slave to a bunch of passing Midianites. Thus, Joseph finds himself being led by a group of foreigners into the far-off land of Egypt (vv. 21–28).

What went through his mind as he journeyed south? He had enjoyed a privileged background as a much-favoured son and went about in his brilliant robe, admired by many. Now he is separated from his beloved father and a victim of his brothers' vicious jealousy. We do not know him well enough yet to imagine quite what is going through his mind, but we can guess that, in his shock and bewilderment, he went back to those dreams. With time on his hands during that journey, he could reflect on those sheaves of corn and the stars in the sky. Perhaps he began to see how it all looked from his brothers' point of view. Maybe he was learning how he might manage those extraordinary night-time insights.

Unexpected turns of circumstance can lead to very productive heart-searching. As the story unfolds, we find that Joseph is able to use the tough times very creatively. The rest of the family remains at the mercy of the mocking monster of jealousy.

Reflection

When you go through a hard time, think about how you can make it a creative time.

MM

Wednesday 16 March

GENESIS 39:1–4 (TNIV)

God with us

Now Joseph had been taken down to Egypt. Potiphar, an Egyptian who was one of Pharaoh's officials, the captain of the guard, bought him from the Ishmaelites who had taken him there. The Lord was with Joseph so that he prospered, and he lived in the house of his Egyptian master. When his master saw that the Lord was with him and that the Lord gave him success in everything he did, Joseph found favour in his eyes and became his attendant. Potiphar put him in charge of his household, and he entrusted to his care everything he owned.

Joseph finds himself arriving in the powerful and sophisticated country of Egypt. On arrival, he is bought by someone who turns out to be one of Pharaoh's senior officials. For the first time in the story, there is a mention of 'the Lord'—we are told that 'the Lord was with him' (v. 2).

This changes the whole dynamic of the story as we are not just reading about a young man fending for himself and relying on his own wits to get him out of trouble. Instead, he has a divine companion and, because of this, there is the implication that it is God who has inspired Potiphar to take Joseph into his household.

'God with us' is at the core of our Christian faith. When, years later, Matthew writes about another Joseph, the husband of Mary, he tells of the prophecy that Jesus is 'Immanuel, which means "God with us"' (Matthew 1:23). *That* Joseph also makes an unexpected journey down to Egypt that seems full of danger yet is safe because of the Lord's presence. As we shall see from our story in Genesis, the fact that God is with Joseph does not mean all is plain sailing, but it does mean he is never alone and that God is influencing the flow of events. That is not to say Joseph is a mere puppet in God's play; it means his latent gifts, such as his dreaming, are empowered, his wisdom is inspired and courage and hope become natural to him. God enables him to become all that he can be.

Prayer

Lord, you are with me, and so I have hope, even in the darkest times.

MM

GENESIS 39:8–10 (TNIV)

Seduced and sentenced

'With me in charge,' [Joseph] told [Potiphar's wife], 'my master does not concern himself with anything in the house; everything he owns he has entrusted to my care. No one is greater in this house than I am. My master has withheld nothing from me except you, because you are his wife. How then could I do such a wicked thing and sin against God?' And though she spoke to Joseph day after day, he refused to go to bed with her or even to be with her.

Just when things seem to be going swimmingly for Joseph, disaster strikes in the form of sex—specifically, Mrs Potiphar's interest in the subject. It has not escaped her attention that her husband's slave is a very attractive young man. As the wife of a VIP, she sees no reason not to enjoy some privileges and, after all, Joseph *is* merely a slave. That, though, is not how Joseph sees it.

He displays here a keen conscience and a strong desire to follow God. To commit adultery would be to break one of the great commandments of his faith and his people. Further, he sees himself as a dignified human, not a slave to be used by others.

For the second time in his story, this young man succeeds in infuriating someone so much that she wants him to be seriously punished. This time it is not his brothers who feel offended, but the wife of his master. She succeeds in tricking him in such a way that it appears as if he is the one who is guilty of seducing her (vv. 11–18).

It must have been desperately disappointing for Potiphar to lose this very capable young man from his household. Joseph knew what the punishment was for an act of adultery—death. Potiphar is extraordinarily lenient, however, and spares Joseph's life, sending him to jail instead. The Lord is with Joseph and will not allow his life to come to a premature end. Joseph risked much to retain his own integrity, but, in the end, he is vindicated.

Prayer

Lord, give me the courage to stand up for what is right,
even if it means that I will be misunderstood.

MM

Friday 18 March

GENESIS 39:20–23 (TNIV)

Prison duties

> Joseph's master took him and put him in prison, the place where the king's prisoners were confined. But while Joseph was there in the prison, the Lord was with him; he showed him kindness and granted him favour in the eyes of the prison warder. So the warder put Joseph in charge of all those held in the prison, and he was made responsible for all that was done there. The warder paid no attention to anything under Joseph's care, because the Lord was with Joseph and gave him success in whatever he did.

I think it is fair to assume that the prison term was life imprisonment, so the early days must have been bleak for Joseph. The wheel of fortune was making him dizzy—from favoured son, in his posh coat, to being sold as a slave, to running Potiphar's household, to life imprisonment. As we keep discovering, though, he is not at the mercy of fortune's wheel—there is another power at work in his story.

Today's passage tells us what a remarkable man Joseph is. No matter what life throws at him, he does not despair because he knows God is with him. That knowledge has a powerful effect on how he views situations and it is forming his personality.

Apart from his brothers, who were soured by jealousy, people obviously like Joseph. There is something very appealing in his character, such that even the prison warden grew to trust him so much that he put him in charge of the other prisoners.

There is also something entrepreneurial about Joseph—no matter where he is, he sees how jobs can be done well and he uses his gifts to get on and do them with great success. In this way, he is truly inspiring.

If we find ourselves imprisoned by our circumstances, we can remember Joseph. God *is* with us, as he was with Joseph, and if we will take that knowledge deep into our hearts, we too will begin to find ways to cope that can eventually lead us to freedom.

Reflection

What do you do when you feel trapped? Dwell on the knowledge that God is with you and ask him for the energy you need to cope.

MM

Genesis 40:2–8 (TNIV, abridged)

Prison dreams

Pharaoh was angry with his two officials, the chief cupbearer and the chief baker, and put them in custody in the house of the captain of the guard, in the same prison where Joseph was confined... After they had been in custody for some time, each of the two men... had a dream the same night... [Joseph] asked [them], 'Why do you look so sad today?' 'We both had dreams,' they answered, 'but there is no one to interpret them.' Then Joseph said to them, 'Do not interpretations belong to God? Tell me your dreams.'

The two officials are in custody awaiting Pharaoh's verdict and they are nervously wondering about their fate. One night, they each have what they know to be a significant dream and both are troubled by them. Joseph notices this and gets them talking about their dreams, an area that he finds particularly interesting.

The cupbearer (or butler) and baker would not expect a lowly, foreign slave and fellow prisoner to be able to interpret dreams, because such a job was normally performed by much more senior people. Joseph, however, puts them right on this by pointing out that it is God who interprets (v. 8) and God may give his gifts to whom he pleases.

Thus it is that both anxious prisoners are offered an interpretation of their dreams, which is great news for the butler, but terrible for the baker (vv. 12–19). Joseph's interpretations prove to be spot on, for Pharaoh reinstates the butler, but executes the baker.

Joseph grows in wisdom during his time in prison. He could so easily set himself up as a grand dream interpreter, but, humbly, he makes it clear that it is God who gives gifts and talents. He is learning that if he uses his gifts to promote his own cause, they lose their value. He has to trust in God for his future and, in the meantime, he knows that he must be a faithful steward of the gifts God has given him, using them in the service of others. This discipline during the difficult prison years will ultimately lead him to the freedom he longs for so much.

Prayer

Lord, thank you for the gifts that you have entrusted to me.
May I use them well today.

MM

GENESIS 41:1, 8, 15–16 (TNIV, ABRIDGED)

Confidence

When two full years had passed, Pharaoh had a dream... In the morning his mind was troubled, so he sent for all the magicians and wise men of Egypt. Pharaoh told them his dreams, but no one could interpret them for him... Pharaoh said to Joseph, 'I had a dream, and no one can interpret it. But I have heard it said of you that when you hear a dream you can interpret it.' 'I cannot do it,' Joseph replied to Pharaoh, 'but God will give Pharaoh the answer he desires.'

It has been two years since Joseph hoped that his interpretation of the officials' dreams would bring him into Pharaoh's favour. The day finally arrives when Pharaoh has a disturbing set of dreams that none of the interpreters understands. The butler suddenly remembers Joseph (vv. 9–13) and he is summoned from prison to interpret the king's dreams.

What I like about Joseph at this stage is his remarkable confidence. 'Confidence' literally means 'with faith' and, in Joseph's case, his confidence is rooted in his faith in God. He senses straight away that the dreams bothering Pharaoh are extremely significant because they have been given to him by God (v. 28).

You can see the scene—Pharaoh in one of those great chambers, the remains of which are still impressive thousands of years on. In front of him stands this young man from a different land who has spent years in imprisonment. Yet there is extraordinary authority in Joseph, which the king immediately recognises and respects.

It is unlikely that many of us will find ourselves brought before royalty and asked to interpret their dreams, but most of us, at one time or another, will find ourselves in situations where we feel way out of our depth and God will require us to use the gifts he has given us to stand up for him and confidently speak to those who have little knowledge of him. The story of Joseph shows us how God chooses to work his purposes through such moments as these.

Reflection

Can you think of a situation where you might naturally feel out of your depth, yet God may call you to share what you know of him?

MM

GENESIS 41:38–41 (TNIV)

The God who lives

Pharaoh asked [his officials], 'Can we find anyone like this man, one in whom is the spirit of God?' Then Pharaoh said to Joseph, 'Since God has made all this known to you, there is no one so discerning and wise as you. You shall be in charge of my palace, and all my people are to submit to your orders. Only with respect to the throne will I be greater than you.' So Pharaoh said to Joseph, 'I hereby put you in charge of the whole land of Egypt.'

At this point, the story becomes truly extraordinary. Such is Joseph's confidence that he not only gives a clear interpretation of Pharaoh's dreams but he also gets into very practical applications (vv. 33–36), urging the king to find a wise person to manage the coming years of abundance and famine. Pharaoh decides to look no further than the prisoner standing in front of him. What persuades Pharaoh is not Joseph's academic qualifications, nor his business experience, but, rather, that he has never seen anyone so alive in the Spirit of God, so he elevates Joseph to being the second most powerful man in the land. He wants to bring Joseph fully into his court circle and so changes his name to an Egyptian one—Zaphenath-Paneah, meaning 'God speaks and he lives' (v. 45). Spiritually, Joseph is completely alone at this time—no one in Egypt knows about his faith, yet it is so strong in him that Pharaoh is bowled over by it.

In much of today's so-called secular society, we can feel alone in our faith and all too easily assume that others will mock or deride us if we dare to share what we believe or testify what the Lord has done in our lives. We can learn from this story, though, that there may well be 'Pharaohs' around who are genuinely on the lookout for people in whom God's Spirit is evidently alive and who are longing to experience the gifts of God in their lives. You may be the one who has a word for them.

Prayer

Lord, grant me the confidence to show others that there is a God in this world who speaks and lives.

MM

GENESIS 41:50–52 (TNIV)

A time to let go

> Before the years of famine came, two sons were born to Joseph by Asenath daughter of Potiphera, priest of On. Joseph named his firstborn Manasseh and said, 'It is because God has made me forget all my trouble and all my father's household.' The second son he named Ephraim and said, 'It is because God has made me fruitful in the land of my suffering.'

Joseph was 30 years old when he became grand vizier of Egypt (v. 46). As if Pharaoh had not honoured him enough, he also gave him in marriage the daughter of the priest of On, the highest priest in the land. Joseph had become completely Egyptian and his former life was starting to feel a long way away. In fact, when his wife gives birth to their first child, he gives him a name that indicates a changed relationship to his home.

The word 'forget' here is misleading, however, because, as the story continues, it is clear that he has forgotten neither his father nor his brothers. What he is able to put to one side is 'all his trouble' and there is a strong suggestion that he has forgiven his brothers for what happened years before. Not only that but he is also no longer hankering after going back. He has accepted the situation in which God has placed him and is not going to spend his energy on either plotting revenge on his brothers or hankering after his lost homeland.

In this way, Joseph shows impressive emotional maturity. As we know, he will have to re-engage with his home life very soon, but maybe he is able to do that successfully because he has reached a point of reconciliation in his own heart.

All kinds of experiences can come our way in life and, even if things are going brilliantly well, memories of past hurts or sorrows can cloud our ability to live fully in the present. Joseph's positive attitude and confidence in God offer us an example of letting go of the past and being fully alive in the present.

Prayer

Lord, show me what I need to let go of, for I want to live
in the fullness of the life you are giving me today.

MM

Genesis 41:56; 42:1–2, 6 (TNIV, abridged)

The dream fulfilled

When the famine had spread over the whole country, Joseph opened all the storehouses and sold grain to the Egyptians, for the famine was severe throughout Egypt... When Jacob learned that there was grain in Egypt, he said to his sons, '...Go down there and buy some for us, so that we may live and not die.'... Now Joseph was the governor of the land, the person who sold grain to all its people. So when Joseph's brothers arrived, they bowed down to him with their faces to the ground.

Joseph has successfully managed the crops during the seven good years and, now, just as God showed through Pharaoh's dreams, the lean years have come and Joseph's task is to distribute the stored grain carefully so that it lasts through the famine. Did his mind ever wander back to Canaan, maybe wondering how his much-loved father was faring? Did he think back to those dreams that so offended his brothers? Did he assume that he would not see his family again?

All that changes now, for the famine has hit Canaan and Jacob decides to send ten of his sons to Egypt to buy grain. He cannot bear to part with Benjamin, though, who remains at home (42:3–4). Thus it is that, one day, Joseph is at the grain market when he sees his brothers and immediately recognises them, even though they do not recognise him, with his shaved head, royal garments and fluent Egyptian (v. 23). When they bowed down to him, Joseph would have remembered those boyhood dreams...

The story would have been a good deal shorter if, at this point, he had revealed who he was. Instead, we enter a very elaborate sequence of hoaxes and guessing games. Part of the reason for that is Joseph is devising a plan to get Benjamin and his father down to Egypt. I also suspect that, in Joseph's mind, is the knowledge that he does not just want to see his family again, he wants to be properly reconciled. For this to happen, there has to be true acknowledgement of the hurt between them. Only then can there be real forgiveness and healing.

Reflection

Think about and pray for situations where you know that reconciliation is needed.

MM

GENESIS 43:26–30 (TNIV, ABRIDGED)

Longings touched by grace

When Joseph came home, [his brothers] presented to him the gifts they had brought... and they bowed down before him to the ground. He asked them how they were, and then he said, 'How is your aged father you told me about?...' They replied, 'Your servant our father is still alive and well.' And they bowed down, prostrating themselves before him. As he... saw his brother Benjamin, his own mother's son, he asked, 'Is this your youngest brother, the one you told me about?' And he said, 'God be gracious to you, my son.' Deeply moved at the sight of his brother, Joseph hurried out and looked for a place to weep. He went into his private room and wept there.

This is the brothers' second journey to Egypt. Joseph had told them that if they were to return they must bring Benjamin (vv. 3–5). For Jacob, this was a terrible wrench as he found it hard to be without Benjamin as well as Joseph, but he was starving and so he had no choice but to let him go with his other sons.

Today's passage is wonderfully human and touching. It is well over 20 years since Joseph has seen Benjamin, with whom he feels a special kinship as they share the same mother. Joseph was suddenly separated from his father and this much-beloved brother against his will, so it is no wonder that he is full of emotion as he sees him again. This tells us that it is no light thing for Joseph to remain in Egypt. Perhaps he has had days of wondering about giving up his senior position and heading back north to see his folks again. What keeps him in Egypt? Is it his successful life? No doubt, establishing his own family is a strong reason for staying. Perhaps more than anything, though, it is knowing that he must serve God and God has called him to a most unexpected ministry in this land that he has made his home.

Perhaps the most telling words in today's passage are 'God be gracious to you'. Joseph has learned much about the grace of God. Now that grace is giving him back the thing he so longed for—his family.

Prayer

Lord, extend your grace to the longings of my heart today.

MM

GENESIS 45:3–5 (TNIV)

The bigger picture

Joseph said to his brothers, 'I am Joseph! Is my father still living?' But his brothers were not able to answer him, because they were terrified at his presence. Then Joseph said to his brothers, 'Come close to me.' When they had done so, he said, 'I am your brother Joseph, the one you sold into Egypt! And now, do not be distressed and do not be angry with yourselves for selling me here, because it was to save lives that God sent me ahead of you.'

Joseph manages to hide his identity from his brothers for a long time, but, eventually, we read that 'Joseph could no longer control himself' (v. 1)—he just has to tell his brothers who he is. He already privately showed emotion when he saw Benjamin, but now he weeps so loudly that people are talking about it all over Pharaoh's household (v. 2).

When he owns up to his real identity, the brothers' first response is to be terrified, suggesting that guilt rather than love is uppermost in their hearts. They expect terrible retribution, but, instead, Joseph beckons them closer. We see here a demonstration of scripture: 'perfect love drives out fear, because fear has to do with punishment' (1 John 4:18).

In the intervening years, Joseph has attended to the wounds of his own soul and been healed by grace, but his brothers have been stuck with the consequences of their jealousy and hatred. As the story progresses, however, it is apparent that Joseph's love drives out the fear in his brothers' hearts.

For Joseph, the crucial thing is that all the events were part of a divine plan: God was leading them out of Canaan to reside in Egypt and he called Joseph there first to prepare the way for others. Despite being so alone in his faith, Joseph has caught sight of the bigger vision and is prepared to do whatever it takes to be useful to God. In so doing, he has developed a wonderfully positive character, forged through both good times and bad.

Reflection

As you look at the circumstances of your own life,
what do you think the bigger plan might be?

MM

Saturday 26 March

GENESIS 45:26–28 (TNIV)

Spirits revived

[The brothers] told [their father], 'Joseph is still alive! In fact, he is ruler of all Egypt.' Jacob was stunned; he did not believe them. But when they told him everything Joseph had said to them, and when he saw the carts Joseph had sent to carry him back, the spirit of their father Jacob revived. And Israel said, 'I'm convinced! My son Joseph is still alive. I will go and see him before I die.'

So it is that we draw near to the end of our story. Joseph and his brothers are reconciled. There is now just one crucial person missing—Jacob, that wrestler with God. Joseph sends his brothers back to fetch him, urging them not to quarrel on the way (v. 24). He knows that old habits can die hard!

Back home, Jacob has been waiting anxiously in a famine-ridden land. His sons have gone off with his beloved Benjamin. As far as he is concerned, Joseph is dead and now Benjamin is in real danger. The champion of faith has become a shadow of his old battling self, until he sees his sons return with this extraordinary news. His son Joseph is not dead. Far from it! He is the grand vizier of Egypt. In his wildest imaginings Jacob never thought that his son's dreams would take him to this destiny. As the old man hears this wonderful news, his spirit revives. He now knows that once he has seen his son well and flourishing he can die in peace.

The chapters that follow describe God telling Jacob that this move to Egypt is part of the divine plan to create a great nation there (46:3), setting the scene for the next epic story of the Bible, that of Moses who will lead the people back to Canaan. For Joseph, the rest of his days are happy ones and he lives to a ripe old age. Before he dies, he does in fact prophesy that God will lead his people out of Egypt and on a return journey to Canaan (50:24). He is a faith-fuelled dreamer to the end.

Prayer

Lord, grant me the faith and confidence of Joseph
that I may flourish in the land of my dwelling.

MM

Don't forget to renew your annual subscription to *New Daylight*! If you enjoy the notes, why not also consider giving a gift subscription to a friend or member of your family?

You will find a subscription order form overleaf.
New Daylight is also available from your local Christian bookshop.

SUBSCRIPTIONS

❑ I would like to take out a subscription myself (complete your name and address details only once)

❑ I would like to give a gift subscription (please complete both name and address sections below)

Your name ____________________

Your address ____________________

____________________ Postcode ____________

Tel ____________ Email ____________________

Gift subscription name ____________________

Gift subscription address ____________________

____________________ Postcode ____________

Gift message (20 words max.) ____________________

____

Please send *New Daylight* beginning with the May 2011 / September 2011 / January 2012 issue: (delete as applicable)

(please tick box)	UK	SURFACE	AIR MAIL
NEW DAYLIGHT	❑ £14.70	❑ £16.50	❑ £19.95
NEW DAYLIGHT 3-year sub	❑ £36.90		
NEW DAYLIGHT DELUXE	❑ £18.00	❑ £23.10	❑ £29.55
NEW DAYLIGHT daily email only	❑ £12.00 (UK and overseas)		

Confirm your email address ____________________

Please complete the payment details below and send, with appropriate payment, to: **BRF, 15 The Chambers, Vineyard, Abingdon OX14 3FE.**

Total enclosed £ ____________ (cheques should be made payable to 'BRF')

Please charge my Visa ❑ Mastercard ❑ Switch card ❑ with £ ____________

Card no. [ ][ ][ ][ ][ ][ ][ ][ ][ ][ ][ ][ ][ ][ ][ ][ ]

Expires [ ][ ][ ][ ] **Security code** [ ][ ][ ]

Issue no (Switch only) [ ][ ][ ][ ]

Signature (essential if paying by credit/Switch) ____________________

BRF is a Registered Charity

Wisdom and folly: 1 Kings 9:1—15:24

David was the greatest king of Israel, not only because he was a successful warrior and a charismatic leader but also because he managed to build the twelve tribes into a united nation. He lived about 1000 years before Christ, but, for the whole of that time, he was the only king of Israel whose son inherited the nation. God had promised him that he would never lack a successor to sit on the throne of Israel, but the chapters we will read during the next fortnight tell the sad story of how human weakness, folly and disobedience meant that the promise could only be partially fulfilled.

There were high hopes for David's son, Solomon, who famously asked God for wisdom rather than riches or power—and his wish was granted. For many years he was a spectacularly successful monarch, known and respected not only for his wisdom but also for his enormous riches, prosperity and military power. He completed the building of the magnificent temple in Jerusalem and was central to the service of dedication recorded in chapter 8.

All seemed set fair, but the 'wise' king later fell prey to what is known as hubris. Its dictionary definition is 'excessive pride or self-confidence', but its original Greek meaning is more relevant here—'presumption towards or defiance of the gods'. Solomon's story is a desperately sad one: God's gifts received, enjoyed and then misused. Even sadder was the consequence for the nation of which he was the head, for Israel would never again be a single people under one king.

God's promise to David was partly fulfilled, however, in that Solomon's descendants retained a foothold of power, ruling the southern tribes of Judah and Benjamin and centred on Jerusalem. The northern ten tribes formed an independent kingdom known simply as 'Israel'. So it remained for six centuries, the occasional good king of Israel or Judah outnumbered by those who 'did what was evil in the sight of the Lord'. Eventually, first the Greeks and then the Romans conquered the whole land and, finally, a true 'son of David' was born—at Bethlehem.

David Winter

Sunday 27 March

1 KINGS 9:1–3 (NRSV)

The house of the Lord

When Solomon had finished building the house of the Lord and the king's house and all that Solomon desired to build, the Lord appeared to Solomon a second time, as he had appeared to him at Gibeon. The Lord said to him, 'I have heard your prayer and your plea, which you made before me; I have consecrated this house that you have built, and put my name there for ever; my eyes and my heart will be there for all time.'

We pick up the story of Solomon, king of Israel, at the high point of his monarchy. He came to the throne in a blaze of public expectation and with a promise from God that his request for wisdom would be answered. Indeed, because that was all he had asked for, not wealth, power or military success, he would receive those, too.

That promise was made to him when the Lord 'appeared' to him on a previous occasion (1 Kings 3:5). Now, the Lord—Yahweh, the God of Abraham, Isaac and Jacob—appears to him again after the dedication of the temple. God had not allowed David to build it because of his sin in relation to Bathsheba and Uriah, although he had cherished the hope of creating a permanent 'house of the Lord'. That privilege was reserved for his son, whose prayers at its magnificent dedication had been heard. God would indeed be with him and the people of Israel and the symbol of that presence would be the temple, in the midst of Jerusalem.

Solomon had prayed that God would be with the people in times of war, famine and drought, ready to forgive them as they repented their sins and restore their fortunes. He had also prayed that they would be compassionate towards their captives and respect the faith of others who pray 'towards this house' (8:42). It is a remarkable prayer—generous and humble, setting noble and lofty aims for the king and his people.

Reflection

God had heard the prayer, but, in the years that lie ahead,
will the king and his people be able to live up
to what God requires of them?

DW

1 KINGS 9:4–5 (NRSV)

The divine carrot

'As for you, if you will walk before me, as David your father walked, with integrity of heart and uprightness, doing according to all that I have commanded you, and keeping my statutes and my ordinances, then I will establish your royal throne over Israel for ever, as I promised your father David, saying, "There shall not fail you a successor on the throne of Israel."'

Solomon had received the gift of wisdom from God. In Hebrew thought, it is not the same as intelligence, knowledge or skill (though someone possessing it might have those qualities as well). It is about judgment, insight and understanding—especially understanding of the ways and will of God.

No less than eight times in three different books of Hebrew scripture (the Old Testament) are we told that 'the fear of the Lord is the beginning of wisdom'. In other words, reverence for God (what 'fear' means in this context), respect for his will and obedience to his commandments are not the *result* of being wise but the *source* of wisdom. The truly wise person, therefore, seeks first of all to know what God, the source of wisdom, requires.

It is that precious gift which Solomon received and here he is told by God that if he uses it with 'integrity of heart and uprightness' and keeps all that God has commanded him, then his reign will not only be blessed by God but also its future—through his successors—will be secure.

That is the promise God sets before him—a kind of spiritual 'carrot', if you like, to encourage him to use his precious gift of wisdom in order to understand the ways and will of God, walk in his 'ways' and obey his will. If he does, then the line of David, through Solomon and his descendants, will stretch endlessly into the future and the united twelve tribes of Israel will be truly blessed.

Reflection

Many of us know, deep down, that the path of blessing is the path of openness to the will and wisdom of God, but we also know that it is not always an easy path to walk. The rewards of doing so, however, are rich indeed.

DW

Tuesday 29 March

1 KINGS 9:6–9 (NRSV, ABRIDGED)

The divine stick

> 'If you turn aside from following me, you or your children... [and] go and serve other gods and worship them, then I will cut Israel off from the land that I have given them; and the house that I have consecrated for my name I will cast out of my sight; and Israel will become a proverb and a taunt among all peoples. This house will become a heap of ruins; everyone passing by it will be astonished, and will hiss; and they will say, "Why has the Lord done such a thing to this land and to this house?" Then they will say, "Because they have forsaken the Lord their God, who brought their ancestors out of the land of Egypt, and embraced other gods, worshipping them and serving them; therefore the Lord has brought this disaster upon them."'

A basic element of biblical wisdom is choice. We can choose the right way or the wrong way. It is there at the start of the Bible, in the story of Adam and Eve, and in the teaching of Jesus (Matthew 7:13–14, for example). The wise person chooses the good; the foolish person chooses the evil.

It is that principle of wise choice the Lord is setting before Solomon in these words. Yesterday we read the promise that, 'if you walk before me with integrity and uprightness' he and his people would be blessed. Now we have the other 'if' and it presents a sober warning.

If Solomon or his descendants were so foolish as to 'turn aside' from following God's ways, by disobeying his commandments or serving 'other gods', then the most appalling calamities would follow. They would lose the promised land and their magnificent temple would be reduced to a pile of rubble. The people of Israel would be scorned by all the nations. We have seen the 'carrot'—the blessing of a royal dynasty that will make and keep the nation great. Now we see the 'stick'—fail to follow the wisdom I have given you, warns the Lord, and all of this will be lost.

Reflection

The choice is always the same for human beings faced with the will of God: collusion (and blessing) or collision (and disaster).

DW

1 KINGS 9:10–13 (NRSV)

The warning disregarded

At the end of twenty years, in which Solomon had built the two houses, the house of the Lord and the king's house, King Hiram of Tyre having supplied Solomon with cedar and cypress timber and gold, as much as he desired, King Solomon gave to Hiram twenty cities in the land of Galilee. But when Hiram came from Tyre to see the cities that Solomon had given him, they did not please him. Therefore he said, 'What kind of cities are these that you have given me, my brother?' So they are called the land of Cabul [probably meaning 'useless'] to this day.

This apparently trivial account of a friendly king disappointed with a gift from a neighbour in fact disguises a major turning point in the story of Solomon. The warning was given in yesterday's reading—that ominous 'if'. *If* Solomon did not walk, as David his father walked, in integrity and uprightness, then terrible consequences would follow.

The standard had already been set for Israel's future kings, in the warning Moses gave the people before they entered the promised land (Deuteronomy 17:14–17). One day they will have a monarchy like other nations, but there are things that their king must not do. One is to allow any 'foreigner' to take control of any of the land. Another is that he must not have 'many horses' or acquire silver and gold 'in great quantity'. Also, he must not take a foreign wife.

Sadly, Solomon, at the peak of his powers, began to fail in each of these respects. In this incident, he gave to the king of Tyre 20 cities in Galilee, which meant that a foreign king would now rule part of the land God had given exclusively to Israel. Then, here and elsewhere, we read of the enormous quantities of silver and gold Solomon acquires, he needed whole cities for his cavalry (1 Kings 9:19) and, to cap it all, he marries the daughter of Pharaoh, king of Egypt (v. 16). The supposedly wise king managed to tick all the wrong boxes.

Reflection

Confidence in God is a good thing; the assumption that he approves of our behaviour is a dangerous one.

DW

1 KINGS 9:24–28 (NRSV)

The indulgent worshipper

But Pharaoh's daughter went up from the city of David to her own house that Solomon had built for her; then he built the Millo. Three times a year Solomon used to offer up burnt-offerings and sacrifices of well-being on the altar that he built for the Lord, offering incense before the Lord. So he completed the house. King Solomon built a fleet of ships at Ezion-geber, which is near Eloth on the shore of the Red Sea, in the land of Edom. Hiram sent his servants with the fleet, sailors who were familiar with the sea, together with the servants of Solomon. They went to Ophir, and imported from there four hundred and twenty talents of gold, which they delivered to King Solomon.

This passage describes a quite common religious phenomenon—one that many of us know from our own experience. Solomon devoutly worshipped the Lord, carefully observing the offerings and sacrifices in the temple that he had built. At the same time, however, as though oblivious to the contradiction involved, he ignored, one by one, the very commandments and laws that the house and sacrifices celebrated. No foreign wives. No accumulation of vast hoards of silver and gold.

His foreign wife, the daughter of Pharaoh, was installed in her own palace, built by Solomon. The great fleet of ships that the king had built, partly manned by sailors from the king of Tyre's navy, brought even more gold into the coffers of the king of Israel—420 talents, which is about 16 tons of it.

Nobody seems to be quite sure what the 'Millo' was—possibly a citadel or perhaps some kind of hanging terraces. Whatever it was, it was clear that money was no object as far as Solomon was concerned. In terms of economic prosperity, Israel and its king had 'never had it so good'. Sadly, where spiritual wealth was concerned the coffers were beginning to look a bit bare.

Reflection

'Woe to you when all speak well of you', warned Jesus (Luke 6:26). Perhaps we are never more vulnerable to temptation than when we think everything is going so well that, surely, God must approve of our activities!

DW

1 KINGS 10:1–7 (NRSV, ABRIDGED)

Hard questions answered

When the queen of Sheba heard of the fame of Solomon (fame due to the name of the Lord), she came to test him with hard questions. She came to Jerusalem with a very great retinue... and when she came to Solomon, she told him all that was on her mind. Solomon answered all her questions; there was nothing hidden from the king that he could not explain to her. When the queen of Sheba had observed all the wisdom of Solomon, the house that he had built... and his burnt-offerings that he offered at the house of the Lord, there was no more spirit in her. So she said to the king, 'The report was true that I heard in my own land of your accomplishments and of your wisdom, but I did not believe the reports until I came and my own eyes had seen it... Your wisdom and prosperity far surpass the report that I had heard.'

I find it hard to think of this story without humming Handel's 'Entry of the Queen of Sheba'! No one seems to know for sure where Sheba was—possibly the Yemen—but its queen was obviously a powerful ruler who had heard of Solomon's wealth and wisdom and wanted to see them for herself. Needless to say, she was overawed. Solomon answered all her questions and met 'every desire that she expressed' (v. 13). Perhaps that included a son—certainly the former royal house of Ethiopia claimed to be descended from the child of Solomon and the Queen.

There's no doubt that the Queen of Sheba was impressed, but probably Solomon was, too. He seems to have had a liking for exotic foreign women and she would certainly have fitted that description. His wisdom was tested and approved. His wealth and power were recognised and admired—and the Queen added to it from her camel train of gifts of spices, gold and precious stones. It was all very impressive, at one level, but far removed from the heritage of David, the shepherd boy who became king.

Reflection

The chronicler recording these events carefully points out that Solomon's wisdom was 'due to the name of the Lord'. Was Solomon in danger of forgetting that?

DW

1 KINGS 10:8–10 (NRSV)

The Queen of Sheba's judgment

[She said to the king] 'Happy are your wives! Happy are these your servants, who continually attend you and hear your wisdom! Blessed be the Lord your God, who has delighted in you and set you on the throne of Israel! Because the Lord loved Israel for ever, he has made you king to execute justice and righteousness.' Then she gave the king one hundred and twenty talents of gold, a great quantity of spices, and precious stones; never again did spices come in such quantity as that which the queen of Sheba gave to King Solomon.

Ah, if only the Queen of Sheba had really known! She was dazzled by the splendour and glamour of the royal house and Solomon's entourage. Her visit in the story as told here, however, is the final high point in Solomon's reign before he fails to execute the very 'justice and righteousness' for which, she said, God had made him king. She was impressed by his wisdom, but could it by now be more a matter of skill, intelligence and experience rather than wisdom in the biblical sense? The very 'wives' she blesses are to prove the tipping point for his decline. Is it perhaps significant that she speaks of 'your wisdom' whereas, as we saw yesterday, the chronicler is very careful to say that all of this was 'due to the name of the Lord'? It's true that she blesses 'the Lord your God' (and interestingly uses the sacred name 'Yahweh'), but only in terms of the way in which he has prospered Solomon. She was clearly impressed with a God who could bring about such astonishing wealth and prosperity.

An aura evidently still hung around the king, as it often does with people of power. His place in biblical history is indelibly associated with wisdom (the proverbial 'wisdom of Solomon') and glory ('Solomon in all his glory', Matthew 6:29). So far as the chronicler is concerned, though, there remains just one more list of his accomplishments, which were indeed impressive (see tomorrow's reading). After that, the glory departs; the wisdom seems to have preceded it.

Reflection

It is quite hard sometimes to remember that everything we have and every accomplishment of our lives are always 'due to the name of the Lord'.

DW

1 KINGS 10:23–27 (NRSV)

Wisdom and prosperity

Thus King Solomon excelled all the kings of the earth in riches and in wisdom. The whole earth sought the presence of Solomon to hear his wisdom, which God had put into his mind. Every one of them brought a present, objects of silver and gold, garments, weaponry, spices, horses, and mules, so much year by year. Solomon gathered together chariots and horses; he had fourteen hundred chariots and twelve thousand horses, which he stationed in the chariot cities and with the king in Jerusalem. The king made silver as common in Jerusalem as stones, and he made cedars as numerous as the sycamores of the Shephelah.

The chronicler presents Solomon as favourably as truth permits. Yes, he is wise and rich, but the wisdom was 'put into his mind' by God and the riches were largely gifts from those who came to benefit from it.

There is no doubt that Jerusalem in his day was awash with splendour—not only the enormous temple dominating the skyline but also the splendid new palace that he had built for himself. Inside the buildings there were unimaginable treasures of gold and silver. It is barely hyperbole to say, as the writer does, that Solomon 'made silver and gold as common in Jerusalem as stones'.

Hebrew thought regarded prosperity as a sign of the Lord's blessing, it is true, but it also recognised the sin of excess and the feeling grows that Solomon's riches are bordering on that. The list of his chariots and horses, for instance, inevitably draws us back yet again to the warning of Moses that, 'He [any future king of Israel] must not acquire many horses for himself' (Deuteronomy 17:16). We must suspect that 1400 chariots and 12,000 horses do indeed constitute 'many' and the chronicler was very aware of that. He seems to be preparing us for the even more damning repudiation of Moses' warning, which begins our next passage.

Reflection

Power and wealth may be gifts of God, as Solomon's undoubtedly were. They are also seductive, especially if those who possess them forget where they have come from.

DW

1 KINGS 11:1–6 (NRSV, ABRIDGED)

A heart 'turned away'

> King Solomon loved many foreign women along with the daughter of Pharaoh: Moabite, Ammonite, Edomite, Sidonian, and Hittite women, from the nations concerning which the Lord had said to the Israelites, 'You shall not enter into marriage with them, neither shall they with you; for they will surely incline your heart to follow their gods'; Solomon clung to these in love. Among his wives were seven hundred princesses and three hundred concubines; and his wives turned away his heart. For when Solomon was old, his wives turned away his heart after other gods; and his heart was not true to the Lord his God, as was the heart of his father David... So Solomon did what was evil in the sight of the Lord, and did not completely follow the Lord, as his father David had done.

Solomon reigned over Israel for 40 years and it was in the closing years of his reign, when he was old, that his heart was 'turned away' from God. Perhaps it was the folly of age, desperately trying to recapture the glamour of earlier years, or simply evidence of a weakened man, too eager to please all the foreign women around him. There were a lot of them—some may question the wisdom of any man taking on 1000 wives! (The 'concubines' were also wives, but not from royal or noble families.) It was his harem, a sign of wealth and status at the time and also of sexual prowess.

Disastrously for Solomon, as well as his favourite wife, the daughter of Pharaoh, many of them were women from the surrounding Canaanite tribes, whose religious beliefs and practices were denounced by the law of Moses. The shrines of the wives' gods were scattered around Jerusalem, and Solomon himself not only accepted their existence but also actually built them. So, the 'if' warning was fulfilled: he 'did what was evil in the sight of the Lord', failing to follow the Lord as fully as his father David had done. The consequences were inevitable.

Reflection

Solomon himself continued to follow the Jewish faith, of course,
but was also influenced by the beliefs of his foreign wives.
Corruption, sadly, is often more infectious than holiness.

DW

1 KINGS 11:7–10 (NRSV)

The ultimate folly of the wise king

Then Solomon built a high place for Chemosh the abomination of Moab, and for Molech the abomination of the Ammonites, on the mountain east of Jerusalem. He did the same for all his foreign wives, who offered incense and sacrificed to their gods. Then the Lord was angry with Solomon, because his heart had turned away from the Lord, the God of Israel, who had appeared to him twice, and had commanded him concerning this matter, that he should not follow other gods; but he did not observe what the Lord commanded.

In case anybody thinks, in these multifaith days, that this is all a bit narrow-minded, racist and prejudiced, it may be worth pointing out that Molech, for instance, was a Canaanite god whose particular ritual was infant sacrifice. His temple stood near Jerusalem and the appalling sacrifice of babies was still being carried out in the days of the reforms under Josiah three centuries later. That Solomon, the son of David, builder of the temple of Yahweh in Jerusalem, should build a 'high place' for Molech is astonishing and demonstrates the hold that his foreign wives had over the elderly king. This high place, and also the shrine to Chemosh, were destroyed by Josiah (2 Kings 23:13).

The judgment of God on Solomon was that his 'heart had turned away from the Lord'. In other words, his allegiance to God was no longer single-minded or whole-hearted, however much he joined in the temple prayers and sacrifices to the Lord. Despite the clearest warnings and explicit commandments of the Law, and many examples from the history of his people, he seems to have felt that his power and wealth in some way insulated him from such restraints on his behaviour. Meeting the needs and desires of his wives was more pressing to him than doing what God required.

Reflection

The story of Solomon is a warning that those who have received God's greatest gifts are required to remain faithful to the one who gave them. Presumption is a very dangerous sin. 'To whom much has been given, much will be required', said Jesus (Luke 12:48). God had been generous in his gifts to the king, but a day of reckoning was drawing near.

DW

1 KINGS 11:11–14, 23 (NRSV)

The consequences of disobedience

Therefore the Lord said to Solomon, 'Since this has been your mind and you have not kept my covenant and my statutes that I have commanded you, I will surely tear the kingdom from you and give it to your servant. Yet for the sake of your father David I will not do it in your lifetime; I will tear it out of the hand of your son. I will not, however, tear away the entire kingdom; I will give one tribe to your son, for the sake of my servant David and for the sake of Jerusalem, which I have chosen.' Then the Lord raised up an adversary against Solomon, Hadad the Edomite; he was of the royal house in Edom... God raised up another adversary against Solomon, Rezon son of Eliada, who had fled from his master, King Hadadezer of Zobah.

The Lord has already judged that Solomon's heart has turned from him. Now there is the judgment of his mind—deliberately (that is the implication of these words) the king has decided not to obey the statutes and commandments of God, which is a breach of the covenant between God and his people. Such wilful disobedience has consequences. His kingdom—the nation he inherited from his father—will be torn apart and given to an unnamed 'servant'.

There are two concessions, however. Because the Lord promised David that his successors would occupy the throne of Israel in perpetuity, Solomon's heirs retain a limited kingship—just the area of Judea, which included Jerusalem, and the tribes of Judah and Benjamin. The second concession is that none of this will take place until after Solomon's death.

The writers of the books of Kings, who are broadly sympathetic to the regime in Jerusalem, nevertheless recognise this as both consequence and judgment. The consequence is the natural result of Solomon's actions; the judgment is God's. The 'wise' king got it profoundly wrong.

Reflection

It is amazing how often we are surprised to find that our actions and choices have consequences. The Bible's message is that they are unavoidable, but that does not mean they cannot be repented, forgiven and even turned to good.

DW

1 KINGS 11:29–33 (NRSV, ABRIDGED)

A people divided by sin

About that time, when Jeroboam was leaving Jerusalem, the prophet Ahijah the Shilonite found him on the road. Ahijah had clothed himself with a new garment. The two of them were alone in the open country when Ahijah laid hold of the new garment he was wearing and tore it into twelve pieces. He then said to Jeroboam: Take for yourself ten pieces; for thus says the Lord, the God of Israel, 'See, I am about to tear the kingdom from the hand of Solomon, and will give you ten tribes. One tribe will remain his, for the sake of my servant David and for the sake of Jerusalem, the city that I have chosen out of all the tribes of Israel. This is because he has forsaken me... and has not walked in my ways, doing what is right in my sight.'

We now learn the identity of the anonymous 'servant' of Solomon who is to become the new king of Israel. His name is Jeroboam and he learns his destiny on the road out of Jerusalem, 'in the open country', where he is met by the prophet Ahijah. He symbolically tears his own new cloak into twelve pieces and gives Jeroboam ten of them, representing the ten northern tribes. All that will be left for Solomon's son in due course is what the prophet calls 'one tribe', although it is in fact two—Judah and Benjamin—in the territory that includes the holy city.

At about the same time as Jeroboam is named as the future king, two foreign rivals make themselves known, as we read yesterday. The era of peace and prosperity is already threatened. Hadad, a member of the Edomite royal family, and Rezon, son of Eliada, have old scores to settle and doubtless see this period of change and uncertainty as an opportunity to do so.

Reflection

Very soon after these events, the death of Solomon is recorded (vv. 41–43). In many ways he was a great and wise king, but he was brought down in the end by his own self-confidence and pride. It is a sad truth that many of us, like him, are 'wise' to the faults of others, but blind to our own.

DW

1 Kings 12:22–28 (NRSV, abridged)

Uneasy kingdoms

The word of God came to Shemaiah the man of God: Say to King Rehoboam of Judah, son of Solomon, and to all the house of Judah and Benjamin, and to the rest of the people, 'Thus says the Lord, You shall not go up or fight against your kindred the people of Israel. Let everyone go home, for this thing is from me.' So they heeded the word of the Lord and went home again... Then Jeroboam said to himself, '...If this people continues to go up to offer sacrifices in the house of the Lord at Jerusalem, the heart of this people will turn again to their master, King Rehoboam of Judah; they will kill me and return to King Rehoboam of Judah.' So the king took counsel, and made two calves of gold. He said to the people, 'You have gone up to Jerusalem long enough. Here are your gods, O Israel, who brought you up out of the land of Egypt.'

This passage reflects the situation created by the death of Solomon, a situation spelled out in greater detail in the following chapters of 1 Kings. The divided kingdoms observed a fragile truce. The prophet Shemaiah's words were heeded and Solomon's son, Rehoboam, did not launch a massive attack on the northern kingdom (v. 21 tells us that he had 180,000 soldiers ready to invade Israel). Even so, border skirmishes continued and sometimes escalated into open conflict during the following years.

Meanwhile, Jeroboam, in the northern kingdom, feared that his people would be drawn back to allegiance to Rehoboam in Jerusalem because of the appeal of the temple and its worship. To counter this, he committed the ultimate sin, repeating the idolatry of the Israelites at Sinai when Aaron told them that the golden calf they had made was their 'god' who had brought them out from Egypt (Exodus 32:4).

Jeroboam was a disastrous king of Israel and Rehoboam a weak king of Judah. Was this to be the future? Would Israel remain split for ever and would there never be another king like David?

Reflection

'You reap whatever you sow' (Galatians 6:7). This is as true for individuals as it is for societies and nations.

DW

1 KINGS 15:9–14 (NRSV, ABRIDGED)

A true heart in Judah

In the twentieth year of King Jeroboam of Israel, Asa began to reign over Judah; he reigned for forty-one years in Jerusalem... Asa did what was right in the sight of the Lord, as his father David had done. He put away the male temple prostitutes out of the land, and removed all the idols that his ancestors had made. He also removed his mother Maacah from being queen mother, because she had made an abominable image for Asherah; Asa cut down her image and burned it at the Wadi Kidron. But the high places were not taken away. Nevertheless the heart of Asa was true to the Lord all his days.

Here, 20 years have passed since the death of Solomon, during which there have been conflict, confusion and religious compromise. Under Jeroboam, the ten tribes adopted many heathen practices, as we saw. Ahijah the prophet warned that, because Jeroboam had 'done evil above all those who were before' him, evil would fall on his house (14:9, 10). It would not be long before Israel would pay a terrible price for its apostasy.

Things had not been much better in the south, but at last a young king appeared, Asa, who was much more in the mould of David. At last it could be said of a king of Judah that he 'did what was right in the sight of the Lord'. The reforms he instituted, however, show how far things had fallen during the intervening years. 'Male prostitutes' in the temple were a feature of pagan worship, but an abomination in terms of the law of Moses. Idols—forbidden under the second commandment—were now abolished, and the king even removed his own mother from royal office because of her involvement with the worship of Asherah, a Canaanite 'mother-goddess'. Asa did not succeed in removing all the 'high places' (the sites of heathen sacrifice) that had multiplied in the final days of Solomon, but much was put right and the Lord was pleased with him.

Reflection

Solomon's heart was 'turned from the Lord'. By contrast, Asa's heart was 'true to the Lord all the days of his life'. Even if his reforms were incomplete, it was his true heart that really mattered. It always is.

DW

The Passion in Matthew

We begin our readings on Passion Sunday and the two weeks that follow it bring us to Easter, so we are going to look, very selectively, at the events that led up to the death and resurrection of Jesus.

We shall have as our guide Matthew, whose account of the Passion of Jesus Christ inspired Bach's great oratorio, the *Saint Matthew Passion*, and whose version of this world-changing story is, for those who follow the official lectionary, the basis of this year's Sunday readings. Not that there is a huge difference between the way the four Gospel writers tell this part of the story of Jesus, but it is helpful to stay with one of them, so as to see the events from his particular angle.

The events from Jesus' first arrival in Jerusalem riding on a donkey to the discovery of his empty tomb appear to fill only one week as Matthew narrates them, yet that short period accounts for more than a third of his Gospel. We can cover only a small part of it in our 15 passages, so I have had to leave out a lot that I expect both you and I would have liked to include. My aim has been to home in on the pivotal events that explain how the story develops and what it all means. I must leave you to fill in the rest at your leisure.

Note that two passages are taken out of order. Jesus' arrival in Jerusalem is commemorated on Palm Sunday and the Last Supper on Maundy Thursday, so I have moved those stories to their 'proper' dates. I hope that is not too confusing.

Jesus of Nazareth and his Galilean disciples came to Jerusalem for the eight days of the Passover festival and the whole story is set against that background. It was a time of great excitement and tension, when Jerusalem was overflowing with visitors from all over the Jewish world and the authorities were always on the lookout for trouble, especially in the temple courtyard, where pilgrims congregated and teachers set up their stalls. This particular year, the trouble came in a form no one was expecting.

Dick France (RTF)

Sunday 10 April

MATTHEW 20:17–19, 28 (TNIV)

'To give his life'

Now Jesus was going up to Jerusalem. On the way, he took the Twelve aside and said to them, 'We are going up to Jerusalem, and the Son of Man will be delivered over to the chief priests and the teachers of the law. They will condemn him to death and will hand him over to the Gentiles to be mocked and flogged and crucified. On the third day he will be raised to life!... The Son of Man did not come to be served, but to serve, and to give his life as a ransom for many.'

Jesus and his closest disciples were Galileans and this is the first time in Matthew's account that they have made the long journey south to the 'foreign' province of Judaea. Its capital, Jerusalem, was the centre of Jewish religion, but its Jewish leaders tended to be suspicious of Galileans, especially if they came with any claim to religious authority. Jesus knew what awaited him there, yet he went, dragging his reluctant disciples with him. It was not some deranged death-wish, but a settled conviction that it was through his death, and subsequent return to life, that his mission to Israel was to be completed.

Jesus called himself 'the Son of Man', a phrase that reminds people of the glorious figure of 'one like a son of man' who, according to Daniel 7:13–14, is destined to rule over all nations. You can read in Matthew 20:20–27 how two of his followers took his destiny too literally and so spectacularly missed the point of what Jesus was saying. He had come not to be served but to serve. That service was to give his life as a ransom for many.

Jesus' death would not be an unfortunate political tragedy, but his crowning achievement. A 'ransom' sets someone else free and, indeed, through his death others would find life. Centuries of theological debate still have not got to the bottom of what such language means, but without it there is no gospel.

Reflection

What would it have been like to be one of the disciples on the road to Jerusalem?

RTF

MATTHEW 21:12–16 (TNIV)

Confrontation in the temple courtyard

Jesus entered the temple courts and drove out all who were buying and selling there. He overturned the tables of the money-changers and the benches of those selling doves. 'It is written,' he said to them, "My house will be called a house of prayer," but you are making it "a den of robbers".' The blind and the lame came to him at the temple, and he healed them. But when the chief priests and the teachers of the law saw the wonderful things he did and the children shouting in the temple courts, 'Hosanna to the Son of David,' they were indignant. 'Do you hear what these children are saying?' they asked him. 'Yes,' replied Jesus, 'have you never read, "From the lips of children and infants you have ordained praise"?'

This passage follows immediately after Jesus' arrival in Jerusalem, which we shall look at on Sunday. The provocation of his followers' shouts of 'Hosanna' outside the city walls is now compounded right in the religious heart of the city by an extraordinary act of bravado, which starts the Hosannas all over again. Jesus is, for some people at least, a popular hero.

Not so with the temple authorities, though. It was they who had authorised the thriving Passover market inside the great Court of the Gentiles, the public part of the temple's precincts. Who was this provincial preacher to denounce it in the manner of an Old Testament prophet? This is the beginning of the confrontation that will lead within a few days to Jesus' arrest and trial. The man is seen as dangerous.

The children have already seen what the authorities will not see. 'Son of David' means the Messiah and it is only the Messiah who dares assert his personal authority over the temple. Those who knew the prophets well might also have been reminded of Malachi 3:1–4: 'suddenly the Lord you are seeking will come to his temple… Who can stand when he appears? For he will be like a refiner's fire…' A new age is dawning and at its heart is not the Jerusalem establishment, but the prophet Jesus from Nazareth.

Reflection

What would Jesus think of the way we worship today?

RTF

MATTHEW 21:23–27 (TNIV)

A matter of authority

Jesus entered the temple courts, and, while he was teaching, the chief priests and the elders of the people came to him. 'By what authority are you doing these things?' they asked. 'And who gave you this authority?' Jesus replied, 'I will also ask you one question. If you answer me, I will tell you by what authority I am doing these things. John's baptism—where did it come from? Was it from heaven, or of human origin?' They discussed it among themselves and said, 'If we say, "From heaven", he will ask, "Then why didn't you believe him?" But if we say, "Of human origin"—we are afraid of the people, for they all hold that John was a prophet.' So they answered Jesus, 'We don't know.' Then he said. 'Neither will I tell you by what authority I am doing these things.'

After Jesus had thrown down the gauntlet by his bold demonstration in the temple, this question was bound to come. The authorities thought, 'This man needs to be cut down to size.' Their question sounds polite, but it carries a hidden threat: the establishment will close ranks against a self-appointed upstart.

Jesus' reply sounds like a cop out. Why will he not give a straight answer? He knows that they could turn it against him if he made an open claim that his authority comes direct from God rather than from the official establishment. In fact, however, his counter-question, for all its apparent evasiveness, does carry the answer clearly within it.

Jesus was not the first popular preacher who had come to the attention of the authorities. The enthusiasm aroused by the radical preaching of John the Baptist had worried them and John's robust response (Matthew 3:7–10) must have rankled. By refusing to support John, they had already put themselves on the wrong side (as Jesus goes on to point out in 21:31–32) and Jesus suggests that they are making the same mistake again. They could hardly miss the implication that he, like John, came with God's authority, so did not need their official endorsement.

Reflection

Why are people so reluctant to recognise the hand of God in someone else's work?

RTF

MATTHEW 23:29–32, 37–39 (TNIV)

The point of no return?

> 'Woe to you, teachers of the law and Pharisees, you hypocrites! You build tombs for the prophets and decorate the graves of the righteous... You testify against yourselves that you are the descendants of those who murdered the prophets. Fill up, then, the measure of the sin of your ancestors!... Jerusalem, Jerusalem, you who kill the prophets and stone those sent to you, how often I have longed to gather your children together, as a hen gathers her chicks under her wings, and you were not willing. Look, your house is left to you desolate. For I tell you, you will not see me again until you say, "Blessed is he who comes in the name of the Lord."'

All through chapters 21—22 Jesus has been engaged in public disputes with the authorities and the confrontation becomes ever sharper. It reaches a climax in chapter 23, where Jesus goes on the offensive and denounces their failure to see things from God's point of view. The establishment has consistently taken the wrong side, opposing those who spoke in God's name, and now the day of reckoning has come.

Jerusalem's failure will be summed up in the coming destruction of the temple (notice, it is 'your house' in v. 38 rather than 'God's house'), which Jesus will more explicitly predict and explain in chapter 24. It happened, in fact, a generation later, when the Roman armies did indeed 'leave no stone on another'. It need not have been so. Jesus' image of the mother bird trying to protect her young gives poignant expression to God's sustained appeal to his people. Many prophets, with John and Jesus as the last in the line, had called in vain for national repentance. God has still left his people the freedom to choose and they have gone the wrong way.

Is there hope for the future? Only if Jerusalem will change its mind and welcome Jesus as the pilgrims had done on Palm Sunday. Will they? Jesus' words leave the question tantalisingly open.

Prayer

'From hardness of heart, and contempt of thy word and commandment, good Lord, deliver us.'

The Litany, Book of Common Prayer

RTF

MATTHEW 26:1B–5, 14–16 (TNIV)

The plot is hatched

[Jesus] said to his disciples, 'As you know, the Passover is two days away—and the Son of Man will be handed over to be crucified.' Then the chief priests and the elders of the people assembled in the palace of the high priest, whose name was Caiaphas, and they plotted to arrest Jesus in some sly way and kill him. 'But not during the Feast,' they said, 'or there may be a riot among the people.'... Then one of the Twelve—the one called Judas Iscariot—went to the chief priests and asked, 'What are you willing to give me if I deliver him over to you?' So they counted out for him thirty pieces of silver. From then on Judas watched for an opportunity to hand him over.

Crowds had already gathered in Jerusalem for the Passover festival and it was clear—not only from the Palm Sunday demonstration but also from the way the crowd had supported Jesus during the debates in the temple courtyard—that he had a strong following among the ordinary people. The authorities thus thought that it would be prudent to arrest Jesus when there was no one else around and before the festival really got going, but, in the overcrowded city, with many pilgrims also camping outside the walls, it would be like looking for a needle in a haystack. They needed an informer.

That was where Judas came in, with his inside knowledge of where the disciple group would spend the night. No one really knows what made him change sides. Thirty denarii (about a month's wages) was hardly enough by itself to induce him to betray the cause for which he had already given up so much. Perhaps he had been looking for a more practical and less otherworldly sort of Messiah, so Jesus' talk of coming to Jerusalem to die had alarmed and disappointed him. Perhaps the confrontation in Jerusalem made him reassess Jesus' mission, so he was even swinging towards the official view that Jesus was a false teacher and a danger to national morale and security?

Reflection

How secure is your loyalty to Jesus and his cause?

RTF

Friday 15 April

MATTHEW 26:31–35 (TNIV)

Loyalty under threat

> Then Jesus told them, 'This very night you will all fall away on account of me, for it is written: "I will strike the shepherd, and the sheep of the flock will be scattered." But after I have risen, I will go ahead of you into Galilee.' Peter replied, 'Even if all fall away on account of you, I never will.' 'Truly I tell you,' Jesus answered, 'this very night, before the cock crows, you will disown me three times.' But Peter declared, 'Even if I have to die with you, I will never disown you.' And all the other disciples said the same.

We will postpone looking at the Last Supper until next Thursday, so, in today's passage, we have jumped to what follows it, as Jesus and the disciples make their way to Gethsemane, outside the city walls. Jesus has warned them that there is a traitor among them (vv. 21–25), but now the loyalty of each one of them comes under scrutiny.

The mention of a traitor has put them all on their mettle. Peter, never slow to take the lead, is sure his loyalty will not crack. We know that it will and we shall read his sorry story next week. I do not think that Peter was insincere, just unaware of his own weakness under pressure. After all, it is easy to be sure of your loyalty when you are among friends.

Jesus knew better. There is sadness, even reproach, in his words, but he has to leave them to find out for themselves. Already, though, even with this gloomy prospect before them, he is looking beyond it all: 'After I have risen, I will go ahead of you.' Not only is there a future but they are also still part of it. Jerusalem, with all its menace and hostility, will be left behind and they will be back in Galilee, where the good news of the kingdom of God first began its triumphant progress. Thus, the scene is set for the astonishing climax of Matthew's story on a mountain in Galilee (28:16–20).

Reflection

'If you think you are standing firm, be careful that you don't fall!'
(1 Corinthians 10:12)

RTF

MATTHEW 26:37–39, 42 (TNIV)

'Your will be done'

He took Peter and the two sons of Zebedee along with him, and he began to be sorrowful and troubled. Then he said to them, 'My soul is overwhelmed with sorrow to the point of death. Stay here and keep watch with me.' Going a little farther, he fell with his face to the ground and prayed, 'My Father, if it is possible, may this cup be taken from me. Yet not as I will, but as you will.'… He went away a second time and prayed, 'My Father, if it is not possible for this cup to be taken away unless I drink it, may your will be done.'

The scene is familiar to us: Jesus' prayer repeated three times and the disciples' failure three times to stay awake and support him. When Judas arrives with the arresting party the disciples are found unprepared and they all desert him, as Jesus had predicted.

The central figure in this scene is Jesus himself. He has spoken with such determination about his coming death that it is a shock to see him now apparently unable to face it. Some have compared this scene unfavourably with Socrates calmly accepting his execution, but this is quite different. Not only is Jesus facing an excruciating form of execution but he also knows that his death is to be 'as a ransom for many' (20:28). His identification with the world's sin will even affect his relationship with the one whom he addresses here as 'my Father', as we shall see in our Good Friday passage. It is, I believe, the prospect of that dire experience which underlies this repeated prayer. Is there no other way?

For all its agony, this is not a 'bottling out' prayer. If this really is his Father's will, so be it. We can hardly begin to imagine what that prayer cost Jesus. His request to be spared the 'cup' remains unanswered because, as he has already insisted, his death is not a political accident but the necessary means to a divinely ordained end.

Reflection

We say in the Lord's Prayer, 'Your will be done.'
Isn't that rather scary?

RTF

MATTHEW 21:8–11 (TNIV)

The prophet from the north

A very large crowd spread their cloaks on the road, while others cut branches from the trees and spread them on the road. The crowds that went ahead of him and those that followed shouted, 'Hosanna to the Son of David!' 'Blessed is he who comes in the name of the Lord!' 'Hosanna in the highest heaven!' When Jesus entered Jerusalem, the whole city was stirred and asked, 'Who is this?' The crowds answered, 'This is Jesus, the prophet from Nazareth in Galilee.'

For Palm Sunday we go back to the events of Jesus' first arrival in Jerusalem. He rides on a donkey to remind people of Zechariah's prophecy of the coming of Jerusalem's 'king' (Zechariah 9:9) and they get the message. This is a royal cavalcade for the 'Son of David'.

So much is familiar, but have you noticed who is shouting 'Hosanna!'? Jesus and his Galilean supporters are arriving as part of a crowd of Passover pilgrims, no doubt many of them also Galileans, who have accompanied him on the road up from Jericho. It is 'the crowds that went ahead of him and those that followed' who are doing the shouting, still outside the city walls.

It is a different story when they enter the city. 'Who is this?' ask the people of Jerusalem. For them, Jesus is an unknown northerner and the shouts of his supporters would have been as welcome to the people of Jerusalem as a crowd of football fans arriving at their oldest rival's home ground (think Everton and Liverpool). The response of the pilgrim crowd simply rubs it in, though: 'This is *our* prophet, and he comes from Nazareth in Galilee'—an obscure village in a suspect northern province, which is hardly the pedigree for a good Jewish prophet, still less for a supposed Messiah.

This divided response is the background for the stand-off in the temple courtyard that we looked at last week. Not everyone, then, is pleased to see the Galilean prophet. Before long some of them will be shouting for his blood.

Reflection

'Hosanna!' and 'Crucify him!'—two shouts, only a few days apart. What made the difference between the two crowds?

RTF

Jesus on trial

Jesus remained silent. The high priest said to him, 'I charge you under oath by the living God: tell us if you are the Messiah, the Son of God.' 'You have said so,' Jesus replied. 'But I say to all of you: from now on you will see the Son of Man sitting at the right hand of the Mighty One and coming on the clouds of heaven.' Then the high priest tore his clothes and said, 'He has spoken blasphemy! Why do we need any more witnesses? Look, now you have heard the blasphemy. What do you think?' 'He is worthy of death,' they answered.

Jesus is difficult to convict, because he will not answer any of the charges. So, the high priest here makes a last desperate effort to break his silence. This time the question goes to the heart of Jesus' mission and he is ready enough with an answer. His enigmatic words, 'You have said so', give a positive but qualified response: the titles are right, but Jesus does not mean by them what the high priest means as he is not merely claiming Jewish leadership.

So it is that Jesus goes on the offensive and spells out what his mission really is. It is, as he later says to Pilate, 'not of this world' (John 18:36). The 'Son of Man' is, in Daniel 7:13–14, one who shares God's heavenly rule. As such, Jesus wields an authority far above that of a mere high priest. Soon they 'will see' him not as their prisoner but as their judge.

His is not diplomatic language and Jesus' defiance provokes the inevitable backlash. For a helpless prisoner to claim supreme authority is not merely ludicrous, it is also outrageous. No mere mortal would dare claim to sit at God's right hand. That is blasphemy—unless, of course, it is true and none of them is prepared to allow for that possibility.

Blasphemy was a capital offence, so the priestly court had the verdict it wanted. It should not be difficult to persuade the Roman governor to execute a man who has made such grandiose claims.

Reflection

'My kingdom is not of this world.' Do people still need to be reminded of this?

RTF

Tuesday 19 April

MATTHEW 26:69–75 (TNIV, ABRIDGED)

Peter on trial

Now Peter was sitting out in the courtyard, and a servant-girl came to him. 'You also were with Jesus of Galilee,' she said. But he denied it before them all. 'I don't know what you're talking about,' he said. Then he went out to the gateway, where another servant-girl saw him and said to the people there, 'This fellow was with Jesus of Nazareth.' He denied it again, with an oath: 'I don't know the man!' After a little while, those sitting there went up to Peter and said, 'Surely you are one of them; your accent gives you away.' Then he began to call down curses, and he swore to them, 'I don't know the man!' Immediately a cock crowed... And he went outside and wept bitterly.

Peter's Galilean accent would have stuck out like a sore thumb in this Judean company—notice the local girl's sneer in the words 'Jesus of Galilee'. Peter, feeling outnumbered, tries to bluster his way out of trouble. It would have been dangerous to know a man who was about to be executed for blasphemy.

There is a parallel between the escalation in the three challenges and in Peter's three responses. First, it is a single servant-girl, then another servant-girl who draws in the bystanders, then the whole group of them. Peter first shrugs off the challenge, then issues an explicit denial under oath and finally goes even further. The rather vague translation 'call down curses' hides a more shameful reality: the Greek verb in the original means to curse *somebody* and, in this setting, probably means that Peter was pressurised into actually cursing Jesus.

Peter's abject failure is in striking contrast with the behaviour of his master, who, on trial for his life, issued a boldly unapologetic challenge to his judges. Peter's disloyalty is not on a level with Judas' treachery, however. That was a settled plan, coolly executed and represented a complete volte-face, whereas Peter's was a temporary lapse under pressure, followed by his immediate remorse. For Judas, there was to be no way back (27:3–10), but Peter would soon be back among the remaining eleven disciples, repentant and restored.

Prayer

Lead us not into temptation; but deliver us from evil.

RTF

MATTHEW 27:15–17, 20–22, 26 (TNIV)

Which Jesus?

Now it was the governor's custom at the Feast to release a prisoner chosen by the crowd. At that time they had a well-known prisoner whose name was Jesus Barabbas. So when the crowd had gathered, Pilate asked them, 'Which one do you want me to release to you: Jesus Barabbas or Jesus who is called the Messiah?'... The chief priests and the elders persuaded the crowd to ask for Barabbas and to have Jesus executed. 'Which of the two do you want me to release to you?' asked the governor. 'Barabbas,' they answered. 'What shall I do, then, with Jesus who is called the Messiah?' Pilate asked. They all answered, 'Crucify him!'... Then he released Barabbas to them. But he had Jesus flogged, and handed him over to be crucified.

Jesus (Greek for Joshua) was one of the commonest names in first-century Palestine and the fact that both prisoners had the same name makes this the story of a choice between two Jesuses. Perhaps Pilate even got the two confused. The crowd, however, did not and the people knew who they wanted.

Barabbas was a member, perhaps the leader, of an insurrectionary group (Mark 15:7) and, in Roman-occupied Palestine, that made him a popular hero. Which Jesus did they want—the one who believed it his patriotic duty to take up arms against imperial oppression or the one who talked about loving your enemy and going a second mile for the Roman soldiers? It really was not much of a contest.

Pilate, as a foreigner, probably did not understand Jewish local politics. Hearing that Jesus of Nazareth was accused of claiming to be the Messiah, he no doubt hoped that he would be a popular choice for a Jewish crowd. What he did not realise was that the people of Jerusalem had never warmed to this Galilean prophet's claim, so Jesus Barabbas, the activist, was much more to their taste. Unlike the Passover pilgrims who had shouted 'Hosanna to the Son of David!', the people of Jerusalem were happy to back their leaders' determination to get rid of Jesus of Nazareth.

Reflection

Do people still face a similar choice? What determines how they decide?

RTF

The Last Supper

> While they were eating, Jesus took bread, and when he had given thanks, he broke it and gave it to his disciples, saying, 'Take and eat; this is my body.' Then he took the cup, and when he had given thanks, he gave it them, saying, 'Drink from it, all of you. This is my blood of the covenant, which is poured out for many for the forgiveness of sins. I tell you, I will not drink of this fruit of the vine from now on until that day when I drink it new with you in my Father's kingdom.'

It is Passover time and, at the Passover meal, food and drink have traditional symbolic meanings that are explained as the group eats together. The sacrifice of the Passover lamb was the basis of Israel's rescue from slavery in Egypt in the days of Moses. Now a new sacrifice is to take its place—that of Jesus himself—so he gives new meanings to the bread and wine of the Passover meal.

His actions dispel any hopes the disciples may have had that Jesus did not really mean what he had said about going to Jerusalem to die. He enacted vividly in front of them a body broken and blood poured out. By inviting them to eat the bread (his 'body') and drink the wine (his 'blood'), however, he also tells them that his death is to be for them. The imagery is shocking—it sounds like cannibalism! At the same time, it is an unforgettable way of saying that his death, like that of the Passover lamb, brings life to those who are identified with him.

His words over the cup echo Isaiah's great prophecy of the servant of God, through whose suffering and death his people are saved, their sin forgiven (Isaiah 53). Death is not to be the end, however. Beyond it, Jesus looks forward to joyful feasting in his Father's kingdom and in that too his disciples will share.

Reflection

Is it possible to become too familiar with Holy Communion? Try to put yourself in the place of those first disciples at the Last Supper and think, what would they have made of its stark symbolism?

RTF

Friday 22 April

MATTHEW 27:45–46, 50–51, 54 (TNIV)

Jesus on the cross

From noon until three in the afternoon darkness came over all the land. About three in the afternoon Jesus cried out in a loud voice, 'Eli, Eli, lema sabachthani?' (which means 'My God, my God, why have you forsaken me?')... And when Jesus had cried out again in a loud voice, he gave up his spirit. At that moment the curtain of the temple was torn in two from top to bottom... When the centurion and those with him who were guarding Jesus saw the earthquake and all that had happened, they were terrified, and exclaimed, 'Surely he was the Son of God!'

This is what Jesus was dreading in Gethsemane. For the only time in the Gospels, he cannot address God as 'Father'. The words he uses are quoted from Psalm 22:1, but that does not mean his sense of abandonment was any less real. The sin of the world has come between Father and Son, but only for a time—John 19:30 suggests that, before he died, a sense of achievement had replaced the desolation he expresses here. Was it the second cry that Matthew mentions?

Jesus had predicted the end of the temple. In this symbolic act of God, its destruction is foreshadowed, but it also has a more positive message. Through Jesus' death, the way into God's presence is torn open. God's people will no longer need the old ritual to approach him: the one perfect sacrifice has been offered and no more will be needed.

It was hard-bitten Roman soldiers who were the first to get the message, though. Perhaps their exclamation was no more than the product of superstitious awe, but Matthew records it so that we can see more deeply into the meaning of the cross. The man whom the Jerusalem leaders had repudiated as a blasphemer and who had himself felt that God was no longer with him was, all the time, the Son of God, carrying out his Father's will. The cross is a triumph, not a tragedy.

Prayer

Forbid it, Lord, that I should boast
Save in the death of Christ, my God.

Isaac Watts, 1707

RTF

MATTHEW 27:57–61 (TNIV)

Dead and buried

As evening approached, there came a rich man from Arimathea, named Joseph, who had himself become a disciple of Jesus. Going to Pilate, he asked for Jesus' body, and Pilate ordered that it be given to him. Joseph took the body, wrapped it in a clean linen cloth, and placed it in his own new tomb that he had cut out of the rock. He rolled a big stone in front of the entrance to the tomb and went away. Mary Magdalene and the other Mary were sitting there opposite the tomb.

The Romans normally threw the bodies of crucified men unceremoniously on the ground. Joseph's brave decision to give Jesus a proper burial was an act of Jewish piety as well as a mark of his personal support. Only a rich man could afford his own rock-cut tomb in a prime site just outside Jerusalem and Joseph's position in society gave him access to Pilate. Even so, it was a bold move to associate himself openly with a condemned man and he could not have been sure that the unpredictable governor would grant his unusual request.

You do not bury someone unless he or she is really dead. Jesus' death was witnessed by Joseph and his workers (a rich man would not have done all the quarrying and burying himself), as well as by the two Marys. Also, the tomb was carefully protected against grave-robbers by the 'big stone' (too big for three women to shift—see Mark 16:1–3). The official guard added in Matthew 27:62–66 made it even more secure. Everyone must have thought that that was the end of Jesus.

The two Marys are mentioned here because it is they who are the first witnesses of Jesus' resurrection. They watched him die (v. 56), they saw where he was buried and they later come back 'to look at the tomb' (28:1). This continuity of witness rules out the suggestion sometimes floated that it was a different tomb they found empty two days later.

Reflection

Jesus said that he would rise again. Do you think Joseph and the two Marys really expected that?

RTF

MATTHEW 28:1–2, 5–10 (TNIV, ABRIDGED)

'He is not here'

After the Sabbath, at dawn on the first day of the week, Mary Magdalene and the other Mary went to look at the tomb. There was a violent earthquake, for an angel of the Lord came down from heaven and, going to the tomb, rolled back the stone and sat on it... The angel said to the women, 'Do not be afraid, for I know that you are looking for Jesus, who was crucified. He is not here; he has risen, just as he said. Come and see the place where he lay.'... So the women hurried away from the tomb, afraid yet filled with joy, and ran to tell his disciples. Suddenly Jesus met them. 'Greetings,' he said. They came to him, clasped his feet and worshipped him. Then Jesus said to them, 'Do not be afraid. Go and tell my brothers to go to Galilee; there they will see me.'

The differing Gospel accounts of what happened that morning all agree that there was an open tomb with no body in it, that women were the first witnesses and that an angel or angels explained what had happened. None of them describes Jesus' resurrection: he has already left the tomb. The stone has been moved not to let Jesus out but to let the women in.

The women are overwhelmed by a very natural mixture of terror and delight. Then (as only Matthew records), they meet the living Jesus outside the tomb. The mind-blowing sight of the crucified man alive again contrasts with his reassuringly banal greeting—effectively, 'Hello!' The women respond with affection and worship.

The message they are given for the disciples recalls what Jesus already said on the way to Gethsemane (26:32) and sets the scene for the triumphant climax of the Gospel in Galilee (28:16–20). Notice to whom it is addressed: 'my *brothers*'. The last time they had seen him was in the garden of Gethsemane, when they had all run away, abandoning Jesus to his fate. What future could there be for them after that? Here, though, he calls them 'brothers' and promises that they too will meet him soon. Hallelujah!

Reflection

Can you imagine a gospel without the resurrection?

RTF

Sayings of Solomon: Proverbs 25 and 26

The wisdom of Solomon—don't we wish we had a slice of it? Wisdom might seem like a quality that drops from heaven only on a very favoured few, but is it really or are its seeds right there in our own hearts, waiting to sprout into principles that can guide our lives?

Where does wisdom come from? Not, surely, from book learning. Learning leads to knowledge, but knowledge is not the same thing as wisdom. It does not flow automatically from learning, but is sifted out of experience, experience that we have reflected on. Remember how often Jesus draws people's attention to their own everyday experience, and then helps them to discover the meanings of God within it.

That is what the writer in Proverbs does—and does it very vividly. He draws our attention to the realities of everyday life: the silversmith extracting the silver from the ore; the gossip spreading rumours; the idler turning over in bed for a bit more sleep; glaze soaking into an earthenware pot. He shows us some of the silly things that we do: interfering with other people's quarrels is like pulling a dog's ears in the street just to see what will happen; trying to bestow wisdom on a fool is like shooting an arrow that has been tied to the bow. These are wonderful, evocative images that may make us laugh, certainly make us think and direct us towards the kind of wisdom that helps us relate more rationally and lovingly to God, others and ourselves.

In our relationship with God, we are warned that divine action in our lives is like a refiner's fire. In our dealings with others, we are warned against too-hasty litigation and advised that a gentle approach can often achieve more than an armed intervention. For ourselves, the advice is to be open to constructive criticism and watch out for the signs of gluttony and gloating, sloth and anger.

So, let us try living with Solomon for a week, allow him to hold his mirror up to our own habits and foibles and polish up what we see there with the cloth of his wisdom.

Margaret Silf

Proverbs 25:2–7 (NRSV)

The refiner's fire

It is the glory of God to conceal things, but the glory of kings is to search things out. Like the heavens for height, like the earth for depth, so the mind of kings is unsearchable. Take away the dross from the silver, and the smith has material for a vessel; take away the wicked from the presence of the king, and his throne will be established in righteousness. Do not put yourself forward in the king's presence or stand in the place of the great; for it is better to be told, 'Come up here', than to be put lower in the presence of a noble.

'It is the glory of God to conceal things…' When you think about it, so much is concealed and the challenge of life often is to work at discovering the hidden treasure, the extraordinary concealed deep within the ordinary. Searching out the mystery deep down in things is the impulse that drives all learning.

I watched a programme on television recently about how gold is extracted from ore. Apparently, a cubic metre of ore will yield only about six grammes of gold and even those few grammes then have to go through a very complex and time-consuming process of purification to reach the 99.9 per cent purity that is the international gold standard.

As I watched, I thought about the specks of gold dust there might be for God to uncover in us and how long it would take to sift them out from all the dross. I thought of what must surely be God's joy as he holds the few grammes of pure you and pure me when the process has been completed.

A friend who makes silver jewellery was watching how silver is purified in intense heat. 'How do you know when it has been in the fire long enough?' she asked the silversmith. 'That's easy,' he replied. 'That is when I can see my reflection in it.'

Reflection

May we have the courage to let God hold us in the fire for as long as it takes until he can see his reflection in us and may we know that, all through that time, he is indeed holding us.

MS

PROVERBS 25:7–15 (NRSV, ABRIDGED)

The power of gentleness

What your eyes have seen do not hastily bring into court... Argue your case with your neighbour directly and do not disclose another's secret... A word fitly spoken is like apples of gold in a setting of silver. Like a gold ring or an ornament of gold is a wise rebuke to a listening ear. Like the cold of snow in the time of harvest are faithful messengers to those who send them; they refresh the spirit of their masters. Like clouds and wind without rain is one who boasts of a gift never given. With patience a ruler may be persuaded, and a soft tongue can break bones.

What a difference it might make to our lives, both personally and collectively, if we were to listen to the wisdom that is packed into today's passage.

We would stop to think before resorting to litigation, first trying to resolve our difficulties amicably and through dialogue instead of going to the courts. We would stop to consider how loyal we are and whether or not we are to be trusted with the confidences of others.

We would learn to accept constructive criticism, as something that can help us become more insightful about ourselves and more compassionate to others. We would learn to value such criticism as highly as a precious jewel.

We would understand that wise words spoken in the right tone of voice at the right moment and with an honest intention are much more likely to be effective than a burst of irrational anger and gentleness can be much more powerful than violence.

We would be willing to take the cold blasts of truth, honestly delivered, as life-giving to our own hearts and minds and, at the same time, see that empty boasts are like dry hot air, bringing no life-giving rains.

All of these graces, however, depend on our learning to listen—to each other, especially when the other is not saying what we want to hear, and to God, from whom all our wisdom flows.

Reflection

May our souls walk gently, slowly, reflectively, listening for the voice of wisdom through all the turmoil of our driven, anxious lives.

MS

PROVERBS 25:20–22, 25–28 (NRSV)

Coals of fire

Like a moth in clothing or a worm in wood, sorrow gnaws at the human heart. If your enemies are hungry, give them bread to eat; and if they are thirsty, give them water to drink; for you will heap coals of fire on their heads, and the Lord will reward you... Like cold water to a thirsty soul, so is good news from a far country. Like a muddied spring or a polluted fountain are the righteous who give way before the wicked. It is not good to eat much honey, or to seek honour on top of honour. Like a city breached, without walls, is one who lacks self-control.

Moving stories are told of incidents that happened during World War II. One in particular shows what today's passage looks like when it is put into practice.

The population of a recently liberated town had turned out to watch—and quite probably to jeer—as a convoy of enemy prisoners of war was marched through their streets. As the starved and broken men stumbled and struggled past, a silence fell on the crowd. The initial euphoria of triumph had turned into the pain of compassion. They gazed at men who were close to death and who no longer had the strength to ask even for mercy.

One woman could not bear what she saw. She slipped back into her house and, risking punishment herself, broke the rules, crossed the line and gave a loaf to one of the hungry soldiers. Her action prompted others to do the same and, very soon, many of the housewives of the town were bringing food for the hungry enemy. Sorrow had gnawed at their hearts. They gave the enemy bread to eat and water to drink. They did not give way before the wicked, nor did they allow the fountains of their hearts to be polluted by revenge. They heaped coals of fire on the head of warmongering and they did it in love.

Reflection

It is better to give our bread to the hungry than spread it thickly with too much honey for ourselves, and better to act with mercy than gloat in triumph.

MS

PROVERBS 26:1–5, 8–9 (NRSV)

How to handle a fool

> Like snow in summer or rain in harvest, so honour is not fitting for a fool. Like a sparrow in its flitting, like a swallow in its flying, an undeserved curse goes nowhere. A whip for the horse, a bridle for the donkey, and a rod for the back of fools. Do not answer fools according to their folly, or you will be a fool yourself. Answer fools according to their folly, or they will be wise in their own eyes... It is like binding a stone in a sling to give honour to a fool. Like a thornbush brandished by the hand of a drunkard is a proverb in the mouth of a fool.

The writer is clearly not someone who suffers fools gladly! A foolish person, he warns, is likely to be all over the place, as unfocused as a flitting sparrow, as lacking in purpose as a curse that is flung out without being warranted. Fools are to be treated, then, just as you would discipline a wayward horse or a stubborn ass.

It is unwise, he adds, to take foolish people seriously or else you will make yourself as foolish as they are themselves. They are already likely to think well of themselves, so to honour them with your attention is like trying to shoot an arrow that has been tied to the bow.

I wonder what Jesus would make of this advice. The Gospel writers would perhaps be more compassionate and certainly a bit less enthusiastic about whips and bridles. So what are we to make of it today, in our own lives?

When I read it, I feel obliged to apply it first to myself before I turn it on others. I can be 'all over the place', unfocused and mindless in some of what I say and do. I can be a bit of an ass and not even recognise my own long ears and mulish attitudes. We should not forget that the first sign of foolishness is to imagine that we are wise.

Reflection

Let us remember that sometimes the biggest fools are ourselves, when we take ourselves too seriously.

MS

PROVERBS 26:13–21 (NRSV)

Starving the fires of anger

The lazy person says, 'There is a lion in the road! There is a lion in the streets!' As a door turns on its hinges, so does a lazy person in bed. The lazy person buries a hand in the dish, and is too tired to bring it back to the mouth. The lazy person is wiser in self-esteem than seven who can answer discreetly. Like somebody who takes a passing dog by the ears is one who meddles in the quarrel of another. Like a maniac who shoots deadly firebrands and arrows, so is one who deceives a neighbour and says, 'I am only joking!' For lack of wood the fire goes out, and where there is no whisperer, quarrelling ceases. As charcoal is to hot embers and wood is to fire, so is a quarrelsome person for kindling strife.

Oh dear! We can almost hear the creak as the idler turns over in bed for just another little snooze and struggles even to get food into his mouth. These are wonderful images of that deadly sin—sloth. Then we move from sloth to anger and the folly of interfering in other people's quarrels, flinging our anger around like deadly arrows and picking quarrels for no good reason.

The kernel of today's wisdom for me, though, is at the end of this passage. I remember learning first aid as a child and being told that, in case of fire, it was important to smother the flames, thereby depriving them of oxygen. Without oxygen the fire will die. Similarly, without our gossiping and grumbling, there is no 'oxygen' for the 'fires' of anger. The slander and malice that we condemn in some of our less principled newspapers is fuelled every time we buy or read such a newspaper and is starved whenever we refuse to do so. Wars begin, not in the corridors of power, but in our own hearts. When we encounter a situation that is already ablaze, do we smother the flames with reason and compassion or pour the oil of our own discontent over an already blazing inferno?

Reflection

Let there be peace on earth and let it begin with me.

MS

PROVERBS 26:22–28 (NRSV)

Smooth tongues and false hearts

The words of a whisperer are like delicious morsels: they go down into the inner parts of the body. Like the glaze covering an earthen vessel are smooth lips with an evil heart. An enemy dissembles in speaking while harbouring deceit within; when an enemy speaks graciously, do not believe it, for there are seven abominations concealed within; though hatred is covered with guile, the enemy's wickedness will be exposed in the assembly. Whoever digs a pit will fall into it, and a stone will come back on the one who starts it rolling. A lying tongue hates its victims, and a flattering mouth works ruin.

How quickly and easily we tend to absorb the things that we want to hear and how fiercely we sometimes resist the things we need to hear but would rather not take in. The image of glaze sinking in through the pores of an earthenware vessel is spot on. The gloss of easy praise is so tasty that we swallow it whole and let it get inside us, where it can all too readily begin to ferment into self-satisfaction and complacency. The honest truth that we badly need to absorb, however, we deflect and dismiss when it is unpalatable.

We are reminded today that smooth words can cover a multitude of deceptions. What we hear is not always what we get. When someone wants something from us, their request may well arrive gift-wrapped in compliments, but, underneath the gloss, there may be quite other intentions. Today's wisdom urges caution: not everyone who speaks well to our faces means well in their hearts.

Yet, there is justice in this process as deception is a pit that the deceiver will eventually fall into. When we cast stones at each other, those stones become boomerangs, recoiling back towards us. When we plan harm for others, we are inadvertently preparing worse harm for ourselves.

Reflection

In the spirit of twelve-step wisdom, may God give us the courage to absorb the truths we need to hear, however unwelcome, the strength to resist and block the deceptions and evil intentions that work harm in our hearts, however beguiling, and the wisdom to know the difference.

MS

The BRF

Magazine

Order Forms

Richard Fisher writes...

By the time you read this, I hope you'll already be aware that 2011 marks the 400th anniversary of the publication of the King James Version (KJV) of the Bible. It promises to be a very significant year for BRF and, indeed, everyone involved in Bible ministry of all kinds, with the anniversary prompting a year-long celebration of the Bible in English.

While we're involved in general terms with the initiatives being championed by both The 2011 Trust (www.2011trust.org.uk) and BibleFresh (www.biblefresh.com), BRF is making a key contribution through our Barnabas in Schools team. We believe 2011 provides a unique opportunity for teachers and children in primary schools to revisit the widespread impact of the Bible on life in the UK. The Bible's significant contribution in the fields of literature, art, music, politics, education, morals and the laws of our land can't be overestimated. This amounts to a compelling educational reason for exploring and celebrating its importance during this anniversary year.

Under the title 'What's so special about the Bible?' we're offering a new resource to schools. This includes a new INSET session for teachers, looking at what sort of book the Bible is and ways to use the Bible creatively in the classroom; a new, interactive Barnabas RE Day for children, using a range of creative arts that explore the Christian's special book; and publication of a set of free resources (including a handbook entitled *The People's Bible* and a DVD) that provide lesson outlines, ideas for collective worship and project material.

The INSET session has been available since September 2010, when the new academic year began, and the RE Day is available to schools throughout 2011. Our hope is to enable even more teachers and primary school children than ever to explore what's so special about the Bible during the year ahead.

Please pray especially for the Barnabas in Schools team during 2011. Take a look at the 2011 Trust and BibleFresh websites, where you will find the latest news about all that's going on, and do encourage your own church to get involved. It's going to be an exciting year!

Richard Fisher, Chief Executive

Messy Church migrates

Lucy Moore

The freezing weather in the UK at the beginning of 2010 made me realise why swallows whizz off to the south, and why so many Brits buy homes in a climate that doesn't require the wearing of vests. Of course, one issue for ex-pats and swallows alike is the thorny one of settling into the new place and making it home—how closely to stick with your own habits and how much to change to fit the surrounding culture. It's interesting to think of Messy Church in this context, too. How much should it try to stay the same wherever it goes and how much should it adapt to local situations?

In February 2010, I joined the Archdeaconry of Gibraltar at their Synod in the Algarve. I have to confess to knowing very little about the Diocese of Europe apart from exotic adverts in the *Church Times* asking for vicars in places like Tenerife or Casablanca—which would be thrust under my husband Paul's nose with pleas that he might be called to somewhere similarly sunny next time we move. It hasn't happened yet. But at the Synod, there were people with name badges that together would have formed the best part of a Thompson's holiday brochure: Gibraltar, Canaries, Malaga, Barcelona... It was very hard not to squeal excitedly at everyone and tell them how lucky they are.

However, it's not always easy to be a vicar of these highly individual congregations. Congregation members of a chaplaincy are often quite elderly, may be away in other parts of the world for long periods, and can be widely scattered, having to travel miles to their nearest Anglican church. A minister might manage only one visit to a parishioner in an afternoon, as distances are so huge. Certainly communications and face-to-face meetings across an area that stretches from northern Spain to northern Africa (and that's just one archdeaconry) are a challenge.

I had the enormous privilege of presenting Messy Church to the Synod. As I'd been up since 2 a.m. to catch a plane, I don't know that I was at my peak, but everyone was very interested and responsive. I doubt that pipe cleaners have often been seen at Synod meetings in the past, and in an hour we covered a lot of ground, inviting discussion about the whole Fresh Expressions movement and the principles and practice of Messy Church itself. I got the impression that, even though the idea of Messy Church appealed to many people who have a great heart for families of ex-pats, it would need considerable rethinking to work in this different context. It will be interesting to see if there are any developments once Synod members have had time to report back to their respective churches. If nothing else, I was able to assure them of our prayers for them and ask them for their prayers for Messy Churches and for BRF.

After the Synod, I enjoyed a weekend with a BRF supporter on the Costa del Sol in Spain, leading a Messy Fiesta in her chaplaincy and preaching in church. It made me feel very close to our BRF network of readers spread out across the world, and very appreciative of belonging to this wonderful worldwide family of Christ. It also reinforced for me how much we need to pray for each other as we all struggle with different pressures and relish different joys.

Could Messy Church be seen as an ex-pat of the sort (and I don't think I met any in Portugal or Spain, so perhaps they're a myth) who clings to The One Great British Way of Doing Things and refuses to have anything to do with Local Culture? I don't think it can be. One thing we've seen over and over again with the different Messy Churches popping up is the way it can be contextualised to work best in the place where it is being developed. While I would say that there are certain givens if an expression of church is going to be called Messy Church—that it's all-age, that it's for people who don't belong to another form of church, and that it's based on hospitality, creativity and celebration—it does seem to be infinitely adaptable. Revd George Lings of the Sheffield Centre wrote:

Messy Church is important within the current re-imagination of what it is to be Church. Don't dumb it down to kids, crafts and church-lite. It fosters inherent participation by contrast to congregational passivity. It connects across the generations instead of 'sending the children out'.

It offers a holistic vision of church by weaving together community and creativity, out of which comes appropriate liturgy. This is positively different from laying on worship into which the attenders are assimilated. Moreover, its spread shows it is accessible and transferable to many contexts. It has much to teach us all. (My emphasis)

It's most exciting where imaginative and sensitive changes have been made to work in a specific setting: out in the marketplace in Liverpool, on the beach in Cornwall, or in a school in Bristol. As Messy Church appears in different countries, it is fascinating to see how it meets the needs of families across the globe, and to ponder how we can learn from our brothers and sisters overseas.

The changes in technology mean that the far-flung limbs of the body of Christ can be linked not just through prayer but through the lifeblood of communication, too. As I'm writing this, I've stopped for 25 minutes to have a Skype call with Debbie Smith in New Zealand. It's 9.30 a.m. here and 10.30 p.m. there—all very surreal, and yet her voice speaking right into my study makes their joys and problems very real. Debbie is coordinating Messy Church for us in New Zealand and is keeping us in touch with the various Messy initiatives that are growing out there. She meets regularly with Jo Latham from Christchurch, who has probably been running her Families @ 4 Messy Church longer than anyone on that side of the world. Jo Skyped recently, too, about the developments they've been making with regard to discipleship:

We struggle with it too. One thing that developed last year was a small coffee morning for four of the mums with their kids who are really getting to know each other and talk together about life issues. Our hope is to gently introduce a low-key study with a grandma who is going to share her story with them first. Another little development that has grown out of the desire to build community among the parents is a home group on a Sunday lunchtime once a month for the whole family, where the kids will be occupied while the parents have a study-cum-discussion, and then on another evening a study for those who are further on the journey. And there's a blokes' event that has helped them get to know each other. All small, with lots of time and energy to grow.

In Canada, our dear Regional Coordinators, Thomas Brauer and Andy and Sue Kalbfleisch, have been enthusiastically sharing the ideas with churches there and working with Fresh Expressions to build up the Messy Churches. Sue reckons there are at least eight in Eastern Canada already, and we know of others right over to the Diocese of Westminster in the west. They grow in a haphazard way, as and when people hear about them, mostly through word of mouth, much as has been happening in the UK.

In Denmark, however, the Lutheran Church read about Messy Church in the book, then got excited enough to have the book translated and to get a website designed and in place before a single Danish Messy Church existed. Bjarne Gertz Olsen was delighted to tell us of three that have started up in the four months since the launch of the book, all encouraged by the Church from the centre.

In South Africa, one lone Messy Church operates, the organiser having heard of it through her contacts in England. Jean Pienaar wrote:

Our Messy Christmas went off remarkably well in December, and all the people (young and old) enjoyed themselves more than they thought they would! It was intentional to keep it small, especially as a 'trial run', and we had about 25 folk enjoy the afternoon. Our schools broke up for their summer holiday at the beginning of December, and traditionally Johannesburg is extremely quiet at that time of the year, as everyone flocks to the coast, or home. Most who attended were directly linked to the parish, but we felt that we also needed to let our own parishioners 'taste' the experience so that they can invite friends next time.

In the States, a Messy Church happens occasionally (and hugely) near Boston, where their Christmas service involved packing 187 gift bags to take round to the city's homeless people.

God's love is the same yesterday, today and for ever; the ways we express his love can change from generation to generation, Messy Church being one of the most recent expressions. The ways we support each other, from Newfoundland to Newquay, are both ancient and modern: through Skype and emails, but also through the tried-and-tested faithful prayer of God's people, one for another. So, once again, thank you for your prayers for BRF as we continually seek God's will and wisdom in reaching out through Messy Church and all the other wonderful ways God has given us to draw people of all ages closer to him.

Lucy Moore heads up BRF's Messy Church ministry. For more information, visit www.messychurch.org.uk.

Working for the Barnabas children's ministry team

Jane Butcher

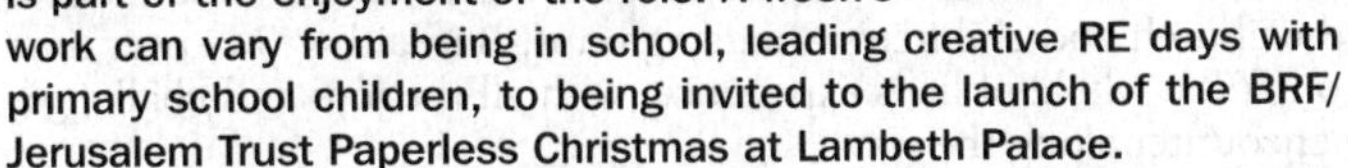

'A week in the life of Barnabas' is a difficult thing to explain. There really aren't any two weeks that are the same—and that, for me, is part of the enjoyment of the role. A week's work can vary from being in school, leading creative RE days with primary school children, to being invited to the launch of the BRF/Jerusalem Trust Paperless Christmas at Lambeth Palace.

It's hard to say which is the most enjoyable aspect of the work. The choices are many and varied—schools work with children, INSET training with teachers, church-based and Messy Church training, being involved with seminars at conferences, networking with other organisations, writing articles and books... and so the list could continue. Every aspect is rewarding in its own way. It is a privilege to hear a child sharing something from his or her faith journey, and equally rewarding to see teachers feeling renewed and enthused after a training day. Likewise, it's encouraging to see church-based leaders feeling equipped for their (often voluntary) role and parents being assured that others are facing the same situations as they do.

Are there challenges? As in so many roles, the answer is 'Yes'. At a practical level, there might be an early morning motorway journey to a fairly distant of the country to reach a school by 8.15am, with the journey home after a long, intensive day of being on your feet. However, one thing can always be guaranteed, and that is the support and encouragement of our fellow team members. We may often be working at opposite ends of the country but the prayer and practical support we receive from one another, and from our many supporters, make a big difference.

We are also aware of the need to keep in touch with what is happening in schools and churches, so that we can tailor our resources to fulfil national requirements, while offering enough flexibility to meet needs that may be specific to a particular church or school setting. Recently, we have seen a rise in the number of requests from churches for longer-term'consultancy' support, which we have begun to provide.

There are most definitely some exciting things happening. Children's ministry never remains static, and we are grateful for that. We ourselves are developing new packages for our RE days and offering new training sessions for teachers, including Quiet Days, which provide the chance to reflect, both professionally and personally. Messy Church continues to grow in new and exciting ways, having now reached as far afield as Canada, Denmark and South Africa.

Another area of work that has been emerging for us recently is 'faith in the home'. There is a growing awareness among many Christian organisations committed to working with children and families that the development of faith in the home does not always receive the attention it deserves. Maybe this is because the church's programmes are focused on other areas, or because faith development is assumed to be the role of the church and children's Sunday groups. But faith grows over time through the whole of life's experience, with all the joys and challenges we encounter along the way.

The Barnabas children's ministry team recognises the need to develop ways of supporting parents, carers and children in their own homes. We seek to offer practical ways to encourage, empower and equip them to work out what it means to be a Christian family in the everyday routines of life. We are committed to researching this area, developing appropriate resources and providing ongoing support for parents' and children's spiritual journey beyond Sunday.

However, we are also increasingly aware of the time pressures that families face, juggling work, school and after-school activities. We know that people are hesitant to embark on programmes that will only add more hours of commitment to an already overstretched family life. For that reason, we want to encourage families to experience 'God in the everyday'. We are seeking to do this with those who have an established Christian faith and want to nurture it at home, as well as the increasing number of people who have not grown up with any experience of the Christian faith and those who just beginning to encounter faith through fresh expressions of church such as Messy Church.

If you are interested in this area of our work, do take the opportunity to look at the Barnabas in Churches website, www.barnabasinchurches.org.uk, and select the Faith at Home tab.

Jane Butcher is a member of the Barnabas children's ministry team, and is based in the Midlands.

Recommended reading

Naomi Starkey

A momentous anniversary falls in 2011: the 400th anniversary of the King James Version (also known as the Authorised Version) of the Bible. It is four centuries since this translation was first published, with the intention of providing a dignified and authoritative English Bible suitable for both public worship and private prayer.

While a great many English translations have appeared since 1611, the King James Version (KJV) remained for generations the most important Protestant version of the Bible and has also profoundly shaped both English language and literature. It is only fitting, therefore, that BRF should mark this anniversary—not least because the KJV is still widely used and loved around the world today. Published in conjunction with the 2011 Trust (established to celebrate the legacy of the KJV), *Celebrating the King James Version* offers short devotional readings by *New Daylight* contributor Rachel Boulding. Drawing from both Old and New Testaments, she writes to help the reader reflect on the richness and resonance of the language.

Rachel also demonstrates that, far from being a 'cultural artefact' or museum piece, this unique and beautiful translation of the Bible continues to speak to us today as we seek to follow God. *Celebrating the King James Version* is primarily designed to be used for daily reflection, but also includes an afterword by Professor Alison Shell of Durham University on the cultural and historical significance of the translation.

Learning to appreciate how the original writers of scripture shaped their text to convey its message, as well as absorbing the message itself, is a significant factor in deepening understanding of how the Bible 'works'. *Meditating with Scripture: John's Gospel* by Elena Bosetti, the first BRF book focused on the ancient tradition of *lectio divina* ('sacred reading'), enhances our appreciation of what many would consider to be the most carefully structured and lyrically written of all the Gospel accounts.

The *lectio divina* way of reading scripture is rooted in an approach that does not separate reason from faith or the intellect from the heart. While understanding the original context is important, fundamental to *lectio divina* is a prayerful listening, under the guiding presence of the Holy Spirit, to what the text is saying to us here and now. *Meditating with Scripture* makes this 'dialogue with the word' accessible to readers, combining exposition of the Gospel text with helpful exercises at the end of each chapter, together with concluding meditations to help shape a personal response. The book has been warmly endorsed by Canon David Winter, who writes, 'This is as persuasive an introduction as one could get to… a way of reading the Bible that lets the sacred text speak directly to heart and mind.'

A meditative reading of scripture is also a feature of another BRF book, *The Promise of Easter* by Fleur Dorrell. This is a companion volume to Fleur's very popular *The Promise of Christmas: Reflections for the Advent Season*, which BRF published in 2007. Like her earlier book, *The Promise of Easter* is published in conjunction with the Mothers' Union, where Fleur works as Head of Faith & Policy. Her role involves enriching MU members in their faith and spirituality and campaigning on social justice and faith issues affecting women and families worldwide.

The Promise of Easter offers non-dated Bible readings and reflections following the themes of holiness, relationship, forgiveness, sacrifice, hope and love, designed to be read primarily during the weeks of Lent. Fleur shows that although such themes are relevant at any time of year, they gain a particular resonance in the Lenten season when we have a particular call to engage with the mysteries of Christ's suffering. Such engagement will bring us closer to our Lord and Saviour, transforming us so that we too may find ourselves willing to offer ourselves in self-sacrificial love to the world. In so doing, we pray that the world in turn will glimpse a little of the true significance of the events of Easter.

Finally, it is exciting to be able to report a further development for a central component of BRF's publishing programme. *The People's Bible Commentary* series was completed in 2006 with Loveday Alexander's volume on the book of Acts, and the series is now established as an important resource for those involved in preaching and teaching the Bible, for first-time students of the Bible, and for those who want to venture into more in-depth study of a passage than is possible with daily Bible reading notes. A number of the New Testament volumes—the four Gospels, plus Acts and 1 and 2 Corinthians—have now been republished as new editions, complete with attractively redesigned covers, to help commend the books to an even wider audience than before.

Naomi Starkey is Editor of New Daylight *and Commissioning Editor for BRF's range of adult books. To order copies of her recommended books, please turn to the order form on page 159.*

An extract from *Jesus Christ—the Alpha & the Omega*

As we pass through the weeks of Lent, the crucified Christ increasingly fills our gaze. However, in order to grasp more fully the scope and significance of his supreme sacrifice, we need to embrace and believe in the whole Christ, Alpha to Omega. In this, the BRF Lent book for 2011, author Dr Nigel G. Wright takes us on two journeys: an extended exploration of the person and work of Jesus Christ, and a journey of devotion and discipleship through the events of Holy Week. The first two readings in the book (both based on John 1:1–18) are extracted below.

Christ the key to all things

And the Word became flesh and lived among us, and we have seen his glory, the glory as of a father's only son, full of grace and truth (v. 14).

A few years ago, I was a speaker at Easter People, the Bible Week initiated by the late Rob Frost. They organisers decided to put me in the alternative venue, where the idea was to do things differently, with more of a performing arts emphasis. The brains behind this venue came up with a new idea. On stage they erected a Christmas tree made of coat hangers. Every speaker was supposed to suspend something from the tree and then talk about it for a full minute without hesitation, deviation or repetition. This was fine, except that they forgot to tell the speakers that this was going to happen. So there we were, scrabbling around in our baggage for something to hang from the tree.

The speaker before me was Adrian Plass, who hung up his toothbrush. I have forgotten now what exactly he said about it but I do remember the toothbrush. Then it was my turn. All I had with me was a bunch of car keys. Inspiration struck: Jesus Christ is the key that unlocks the mysteries of the universe. That, it seems to me, is the great theme that runs through these magnificent first 18 verses of John's Gospel, which are sometimes called the 'Prologue' to John's Gospel. That astonishing belief in Jesus, it equally seems to me, is what lies at the very heart of the Christian faith.

Today we begin a journey together. We do so on [Ash Wednesday], a day that marks the beginning of a pilgrimage Christians take every year, at least in their minds—a journey to Jerusalem, to the cross and to the empty tomb of Jesus. The purpose of our journey is to understand how Christ can be the key to the mysteries of the universe. We shall do this by recalling who Christ is and the journey that he has first made towards us, which precedes any journey that we can make towards him. It is a journey from eternity into time and then from time into eternity. In the church's language, we sometimes speak of God's 'prevenient grace'. By this we mean that Christianity is not, first and foremost, a religion that tells of how we can reach up to God but one that speaks of how God has reached down to us. God has gone before us, coming to us in love and grace in order that we might find him as he draws near. If we ever reach out to God and seek him, it is because his love first prompts us and enables us to do so. Salvation is of the Lord. It comes as a gracious gift from God, as does everything that is good, true and beautiful.

The greatest mystery is the mystery of God himself

What does it mean for Christ to unlock the mysteries of the universe? The greatest mystery is the mystery of God himself. How can finite and sinful human beings speak of God? God is infinitely great, greater than the universe itself, in which there are said to be ten billion galaxies, each containing ten billion stars. By comparison with them, we are so small and insignificant. Our minds and imaginations are all the more puny by contrast with the God who exceeds them all. We might as well seek to contain the oceans in a bucket. We cannot speak of God because, on our own, we have no way of knowing God, no way of unlocking the mystery of God's own being. But there is a key to that mystery and it is Jesus Christ, the one who appears in John's Gospel as 'the Word of God'. 'In the beginning was the Word, and the Word was with God, and the Word was God' (1:1). 'The Word became flesh and lived among us, and we have seen his glory' (v. 14). This is how the Christian can begin to speak of God, because God has first of all spoken to us in a Son who has come to us, clothed in our flesh and living our life.

Jesus is the Word of God. What do we use words for? One way we use them is to express ourselves. Every speaker—perhaps every singer, too—knows that there is something very satisfying about expressing yourself. If Jesus Christ is the Word of God, we can say that in him God is expressing himself; that what is within this mysterious God, who is behind and beyond all things, finds expression in Jesus Christ the Son of God. The Word of God is God's self-expression. We might say that he is the very image of the Father (Colossians 1:15).

That leads us to another thing about words: they communicate. They take what is in my mind and heart and communicate it into yours. If Jesus Christ is the Word of God, he is God communicating God's own self, in order to unlock the mystery of who he is. Because Christ is God's Son, we know that there is a Father, of whom Christ is the image and likeness, a Father who wants to penetrate the darkness and make himself known to us. In Jesus Christ we see the Father.

Those who have seen the Son have seen the Father (John 14:9). Jesus Christ is the Word of the Father. In Jesus, the invisible is made visible. Notice again the words: 'the Word became flesh and lived among us'. In Jesus Christ, the language of eternity is translated into the language of time. God's eternal Word becomes flesh and is clothed in the kind of humanity that you and I can recognise and understand. We cannot speak God's language, so God comes to us speaking in our own. Jesus Christ is the great translator and the great translation of the living God, God's cross-cultural communication. For this reason John goes on to say, in today's passage, 'No one has ever seen God. It is God the only Son, who is close to the Father's heart, who has made him known' (v. 18). This is why we can say that he is the key that unlocks the secrets of God. This is why we should listen to him. This is where our journey must begin.

The Christ who is eternal

In the beginning was the Word, and the Word was with God, and the Word was God. He was in the beginning with God (vv. 1–2).

Our first journey is the journey of discovery. We are seeking to understand who Christ is in his fullness, in order that we may be fully devoted to him. If Christ is the key that unlocks the mystery of God's own being, this can only be because there is a way in which he shares God's being as God. According to our key verse, this means that he was 'in the beginning with God', and he 'was God'. We have to debate what this means. To be with God 'in the beginning' surely refers to the beginning of creation (Genesis 1:1). When space and time were summoned into being, the Word was already there, preceding it all. He was preceding it all because whatever God is, the Word also was. As we saw in yesterday's reading, John asserts that the Word who 'was' then 'became' flesh (v. 14). Something momentous and world-transforming happened: Christ became something he had not previously been—a part of the creation, sharing creation's finite limits and vulnerability, which is what 'flesh' implies.

Before we can make journeys of discovery or devotion, we need to see that Christ has first made his own journey from eternity into time. This clearly marks him out from any other human being. Human lives begin when they are conceived in the womb, but Christ is different. Christ 'was' before ever he was conceived in the womb. In the human being known as Jesus of Nazareth, the Word of God—who has been from the beginning, from eternity, who was with God and was God—has found expression and become incarnate. This means that the Word of God pre-existed the human person called Jesus of Nazareth, became identical with him in the incarnation and in this way became the Christ of God, who is God's saving gift to us.

In all of this, there is certainly a great deal that needs to be understood! Although, for many of us, these may be familiar truths, they can never stop being utterly astonishing ones. To say that Christ shares in eternity turns out to be a matter of the utmost importance. There are those who have tried to explain the importance of Jesus by saying that he was a human being especially favoured by God, even one who had been adopted by God to share in a special divine status. Others have thought that Jesus was created by God as the first and highest of God's works, a kind of angelic or semi-divine figure (although to be 'semi' divine would seem to be a contradiction in terms). But none of these attempts to honour Jesus really work. They succeed only in making Jesus less than the one he actually is, for underlying these apparently difficult patterns of thought there is one massive existential question: is Jesus Christ a human being to be revered and honoured only, or is the Word of God manifest in the flesh to be *worshipped*?

According to the Hebrew Scriptures, which Christians accept as the Old Testament, there is only one God, and that one God alone is to be worshipped (Deuteronomy 5:7; 6:4–5). To worship Christ, if he did not share in the divine being, would be wrong. It might be quite proper to honour and revere him, but certainly not to bow before him in worship, to call him 'my Lord and my God' (John 20:28) and give him divine honour and praise. Yet this is exactly what we find that the first

Christians did, and this is what the visions of the book of Revelation inspire Christians of all generations to do. Here, the Lamb of God (who is also the Word of God known as Jesus Christ) shares both the throne of God and the worship of God as 'every creature in heaven and on earth and under the earth and in the sea' says, 'To the one seated on the throne and to the Lamb be blessing and honour and glory and might for ever and ever!' (Revelation 5:13).

Jesus Christ is the key that unlocks the mystery of God

The eternity of the Christ is actually a quality associated with his deity, his sharing in the divine nature. It turns out to be a key assertion about the person of Christ. God is eternal; Christ is God; therefore Christ shares in eternity. To put it the other way round, Christ is eternal; eternity is a quality of God; therefore Christ is God. To make this claim is not abstract theology but a statement about something that is of the greatest importance to Christians and must be allowed to shape their lives. As we have already noted, without this statement it would not be appropriate for Christians to worship Christ. Yet this is exactly what they do whenever they pronounce the Gloria: 'Glory to the Father, and to the Son, and to the Holy Spirit, as it was in the beginning, is now and shall be for ever. Amen.'

Jesus Christ is the key that unlocks the mystery of God. We can add to that another belief: because he unlocks the mystery of God, he is also able to unlock the mystery of our own lives. He enables us to see ourselves within the framework of ultimate reality or of eternity. It is out of the mystery of eternity that Christ has come, giving a meaning to time. Everybody lives for something. The most thoughtful people know what they most value. It has been said that, strictly speaking, there is no such thing as a 'godless' man or woman. Everybody has something that they regard as their object of ultimate devotion, even if it may not be worthy of the name. It is important that whatever we live for is really worth the love and devotion we bring to it; otherwise we ourselves become diminished. We come to resemble whatever it is that we most honour. For Christians, to honour Christ is to root ourselves in someone who is of eternal value and significance, someone who is worthy, and that can only do us good.

To order a copy of this book, please turn to the order form on page 159.

NEW DAYLIGHT SUBSCRIPTIONS

Please note our subscription rates 2011–2012. From the May 2011 issue, the new subscription rates will be:

Individual subscriptions covering 3 issues for under 5 copies, payable in advance (including postage and packing):

	UK	SURFACE	AIRMAIL
NEW DAYLIGHT each set of 3 p.a.	£14.70	£16.50	£19.95
NEW DAYLIGHT 3-year sub i.e. 9 issues (Not available for Deluxe)	£36.90	N/A	N/A
NEW DAYLIGHT DELUXE each set of 3 p.a.	£18.00	£23.10	£29.55
NEW DAYLIGHT by email	£12.00		

Group subscriptions covering 3 issues for 5 copies or more, sent to ONE address (post free):

NEW DAYLIGHT	£11.70	each set of 3 p.a.
NEW DAYLIGHT DELUXE	£14.97	each set of 3 p.a.

Please note that the annual billing period for Group Subscriptions runs from 1 May to 30 April.

Copies of the notes may also be obtained from Christian bookshops:

NEW DAYLIGHT	£3.90 each copy
NEW DAYLIGHT DELUXE	£4.99 each copy

Visit www.biblereadingnotes.org.uk for information about our other Bible reading notes and Apple apps for iPhone and iPod touch.

SUPPORTING BRF'S MINISTRY

As a Christian charity, BRF is involved in five distinct yet complementary areas.

- **BRF** (www.brf.org.uk) resources adults for their spiritual journey through Bible reading notes, books, and a programme of quiet days and teaching days. BRF also provides the infrastructure that supports our other four specialist ministries.
- **Foundations21** (www.foundations21.org.uk) provides flexible and innovative ways for individuals and groups to explore their Christian faith and discipleship through a multimedia internet-based resource.
- **Messy Church**, led by Lucy Moore (www.messychurch.org.uk), enables churches all over the UK (and increasingly abroad) to reach children and adults beyond the fringes of the church.
- **Barnabas in Churches** (www.barnabasinchurches.org.uk) helps churches to support, resource and develop their children's ministry with the under-11s more effectively.
- **Barnabas in Schools** (www.barnabasinschools.org.uk) enables primary school children and teachers to explore Christianity creatively and bring the Bible alive within RE and Collective Worship.

At the heart of BRF's ministry is a desire to equip adults and children for Christian living—helping them to read and understand the Bible, to explore prayer and to grow as disciples of Jesus. We need your help to make a real impact on the local church, local schools and the wider community.

- You could support BRF's ministry with a donation or standing order (using the response form overleaf).
- You could consider making a bequest to BRF in your will.
- You could encourage your church to support BRF as part of your church's giving to home mission—perhaps focusing on a specific area of our ministry, or a particular member of our Barnabas team.
- Most important of all, you could support BRF with your prayers.

If you would like to discuss how a specific gift or bequest could be used in the development of our ministry, please phone 01865 319700 or email enquiries@brf.org.uk.

Whatever you can do or give, we thank you for your support.

BRF MINISTRY APPEAL RESPONSE FORM

Name ____________________

Address ____________________

____________________ Postcode ________

Telephone ____________ Email ____________

Gift Aid Declaration

❑ I am a UK taxpayer. I want BRF to treat as Gift Aid Donations all donations I make from 6 April 2000 until I notify you otherwise.

Signature ____________________ Date ________

❑ I would like to support BRF's ministry with a regular donation by standing order

Standing Order – Banker's Order

To the Manager, Name of Bank/Building Society

Address ____________________

____________________ Postcode ________

Sort Code ____________ Account Name ____________

Account No ____________________

Please pay Royal Bank of Scotland plc, Drummonds, 49 Charing Cross, London SW1A 2DX (Sort Code 16-00-38), for the account of BRF A/C No. 00774151

The sum of ______ pounds on ___ / ___ / ___ (insert date) and thereafter the same amount on the same day of each month annually until further notice.

Signature ____________________ Date ________

Single donation

❑ I enclose my cheque/credit card/Switch card details for a donation of £5 £10 £25 £50 £100 £250 (other) £ ______ to support BRF's ministry

Card no. | | | | | | | | | | | | | | | | |

Expires | | | | | **Security code** | | | |

Issue no. (Switch only) | | | | |

Signature ____________________ Date ________

❑ Please send me information about making a bequest to BRF in my will.

Please detach and send this completed form to: Richard Fisher, BRF, 15 The Chambers, Vineyard, Abingdon OX14 3FE. BRF is a Registered Charity (No.233280)

 ND 0111

NEW DAYLIGHT SUBSCRIPTIONS

❑ I would like to take out a subscription myself:

Your name ______________________________
Your address ______________________________
______________________________ Postcode ____________
Tel ____________ Email ______________________________

Please send *New Daylight* beginning with the May 2011 / September 2011 / January 2012 issue: (delete as applicable)

(please tick box)	UK	SURFACE	AIR MAIL
NEW DAYLIGHT	❑ £14.70	❑ £16.50	❑ £19.95
NEW DAYLIGHT 3-year sub	❑ £36.90		
NEW DAYLIGHT DELUXE	❑ £18.00	❑ £23.10	❑ £29.55
NEW DAYLIGHT daily email only	❑ £12.00 (UK and overseas)		

❑ I would like to give a gift subscription (please complete both name and address sections above and below):

Gift subscription name ______________________________
Gift subscription address ______________________________
______________________________ Postcode ____________

Gift message (20 words max. or include your own gift card for the recipient)
____
____

Please send *New Daylight* beginning with the May 2011 / September 2011 / January 2012 issue: (delete as applicable)

(please tick box)	UK	SURFACE	AIR MAIL
NEW DAYLIGHT	❑ £14.70	❑ £16.50	❑ £19.95
NEW DAYLIGHT 3-year sub	❑ £36.90		
NEW DAYLIGHT DELUXE	❑ £18.00	❑ £23.10	❑ £29.55
NEW DAYLIGHT daily email only	❑ £12.00 (UK and overseas)		

Please complete your payment details overleaf.

BRF is a Registered Charity

SUBSCRIPTION PAYMENT DETAILS

Please complete the payment details below and send with appropriate payment and completed Subscriptions order form to:

BRF, 15 The Chambers, Vineyard, Abingdon OX14 3FE

Total enclosed £ ____________ (cheques should be made payable to 'BRF')

Please charge my Visa ❑ Mastercard ❑ Switch card ❑ with £ __________

Card no: | | | | | | | | | | | | | | | | |

Expires | | | | | Security code | | | |

Issue no (Switch only) | | | | |

Signature (essential if paying by credit/Switch) ______________________________

❑ Please do not send me further information about BRF publications.

BRF is a Registered Charity